D0238716

50 Walks in

SURREY

First published 2001
Researched and written by David Foster

Produced by AA Publishing
© Automobile Association Developments Limited 2001
Illustrations © Automobile Association Developments Limited 2001

Published by AA Publishing (a trading name of Automobile Association Developments Limited, whose registered office is Norfolk House, Priestley Road, Basingstoke, Hampshire RG24 9NY; registered number 1878835)

ObOS Ordnance Survey This product includes mapping data licensed from Ordnance Survey® with the permission of the Controller of Her Majesty's Stationery Office.
© Crown copyright 2001. All rights reserved. Licence number 399221

ISBN 0 7495 2875 3

A CIP catalogue record for this book is available from the British Library.

The contents of this book are believed correct at the time of printing. Nevertheless, the publishers cannot be held responsible for any errors or omissions or for changes in the details given in this book or for the consequences of any reliance on the information it provides. We have tried to ensure accuracy in this book, but things do change and we would be grateful if readers would advise us of any inaccuracies they may encounter.

We have taken all reasonable steps to ensure that these walks are safe and achievable by walkers with a realistic level of fitness. However, all outdoor activities involve a degree of risk and the publishers accept no responsibility for any injuries caused to readers whilst following these walks. For more advice on walking safely see page 128.

Visit the AA Publishing website at www.theAA.com

Paste-up and editorial by Outcrop Publishing Services for AA Publishing

Colour reproduction by LC Repro
Printed in Italy by Rotolito Lombarda Spa

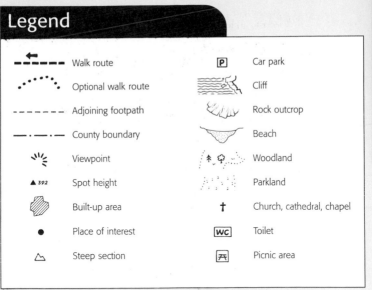

Legend

◄–·–·–·–	Walk route	P	Car park
••••••	Optional walk route	≈≈≈	Cliff
– – – – –	Adjoining footpath		Rock outcrop
–·–·–·–	County boundary		Beach
☼	Viewpoint	♠ ♧	Woodland
▲ 392	Spot height		Parkland
	Built-up area	†	Church, cathedral, chapel
●	Place of interest	WC	Toilet
△	Steep section	禾	Picnic area

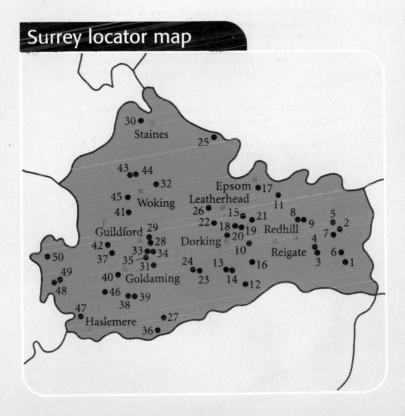

Surrey locator map

Contents

Contents

Rating: Each walk is rated for its relative difficulty compared to the other walks in this book. Walks marked 🚶🚶 🚶 🚶 are likely to be shorter and easier with little total ascent. The hardest walks are marked 🚶🚶 🚶🚶 🚶🚶 .

Walking in Safety: For advice and safety tips ➤ 128.

Introducing Surrey

Somewhere in the depths of Surrey's wilderness I was trudging down an ancient hollow way, gouged so deeply into the landscape that I passed unseen from the woods above. The sides of the lane dripped with mosses and ferns, and tree roots gripped the banks like the toes of swimmers on the water's edge. In the gathering dusk the woods gave way to fields, and the fields gave way to a village where lights were coming on in the mellow half-timbered houses around the green.

Surrey may be better known for its suburbia than its scenery, but the image is unjust. Over a quarter of the county's landscapes are official Areas of Outstanding Natural Beauty, and along the downs and the greensand ridge you can gaze to distant horizons with hardly a building in sight. This is one of England's most wooded counties, and has more village greens than any other shire. You'll find sandy tracks and cottage gardens, folded hillsides and welcoming village inns. There's variety, too, as the fields and meadows of the east give way to the wooded downs and valleys west of the River Mole.

PUBLIC TRANSPORT ⓘ

For most of us, a linear walk leaves the practical problem of getting back to a car at the start. You can't always judge exactly how long your walk will take, and there's nothing more frustrating than hanging around for public transport when you're tired. That's why all the linear walks in this book are back to front. It's much better to drive to the end of your walk, where you can time your arrival easily and catch the bus or train to the start. After that, you're in control; take the walk at your own speed, and your car will be waiting for you when you finish. For details of public transport services in Surrey, ring the national enquiry service on (0870) 6082608; it's open daily, from 7AM to 8PM. You can also find bus and rail information on the internet at www.pti.org.uk.

Of course there are also large built-up areas, mainly within and around the M25; but even here you can still find some appealing walks. On the fringe of Greater London you can picnic in Chaldon's hay meadows, explore the wide open downs at Epsom, or drift idly beside the broad reaches of the stately River Thames.

Deep in the Surrey countryside you'll discover the Romans at Farley Heath, and mingle with the monks at England's first Cistercian monastery. You'll see buildings by great architects, like Edwin Lutyens and Sir George Gilbert Scott, and meet authors too, from John Donne to Agatha Christie. Then, amongst a host of curiosities, you'll unearth London's lost route to the sea, and find out how information technology put Chatley on line fully 15 years before Queen Victoria ascended the throne.

Six long distance routes, including two National Trails, weave their way around the county, and you'll sample sections of all of them as you journey through these pages. The Thames Path needs no introduction on its Royal progress from Runnymede to Hampton Court. Next comes the North Downs Way, linking Farnham with Canterbury and Dover; a little further south, the Greensand Way runs east along the glorious ridge from Haslemere. The Downs Link and the Wey South Path follow disused rail and canal routes south from Guildford, connecting Surrey with the South Downs Way. Finally, the Sussex Border Path slips in and out of the county between Haslemere and East Grinstead as it tracks the boundary with Surrey's southern neighbour.

So pull on your walking boots, dig out the maps, and join me as we set out into Surrey's magnificent highways and byways…

Using this Book

Information panels
An information panel for each walk shows its relative difficulty (► 5), the distance and total amount of ascent. An indication of the gradients you will encounter is shown by the rating ▲ ▲ ▲ (no steep slopes) to ▲ ▲ ▲ (several very steep slopes).

Maps
There are 30 maps, covering 40 of the walks. Some walks have a suggested option in the same area. The information panel for these walks will tell you how much extra walking is involved. On short-cut suggestions the panel will tell you the total distance if you set out from the start of the main walk. Where an option returns to the same point on the main walk, just the distance of the loop is given. Where an option leaves the main walk at one point and returns to it at another, then the distance shown is for the whole walk. The minimum time suggested is for reasonably fit walkers and doesn't allow for stops. Each walk has a suggested map. Laminated aqua3 maps are longer lasting and water resistant.

Start Points
The start of each walk is given as a six-figure grid reference prefixed by two letters indicating which 100km square of the National Grid it refers to. You'll find more information on grid references on most Ordnance Survey maps.

Dogs
We have tried to give dog owners useful advice about how dog friendly each walk is. Please respect other countryside users. Keep your dog under control, especially around livestock, and obey local bylaws and other dog control notices.

Car Parking
Many of the car parks suggested are public, but occasionally you may find you have to park on the roadside or in a lay-by. Please be considerate when you leave your car, ensuring that access roads or gates are not blocked and that other vehicles can pass safely.

Walk 1

Power and Flour at Haxted

A lowland walk that tracks the remarkable story of an east Surrey water mill.

•DISTANCE•	5½ miles (9km)
•MINIMUM TIME•	2hrs
•ASCENT / GRADIENT•	66ft (20m) ▲▲▲
•LEVEL OF DIFFICULTY•	🚶 🚶 🚶
•PATHS•	Field edge paths can be overgrown or muddy, farm tracks and country lanes, 15 stiles
•LANDSCAPE•	Flattish farmland in headwaters of the River Eden
•SUGGESTED MAP•	aqua3 OS Explorers 146 Dorking, Box Hill & Reigate, 147 Sevenoaks & Tonbridge
•START / FINISH•	Grid reference: TQ 385435
•DOG FRIENDLINESS•	Poor; farmyards, livestock and traffic will all keep Fido on the lead, and many stiles may prove troublesome
•PARKING•	Free council car park in Gun Pit Road, Lingfield
•PUBLIC TOILETS•	None on route

BACKGROUND TO THE WALK

Even an estate agent might tell you that the small pile of masonry which lies on the Surrey border, a couple of miles east of Lingfield, needs something more than a lick of paint. Once, Starborough Castle was home to one of the grandest families in the land; now, to be honest, it's nothing more than a ruin.

High Office

The Cobham family had lived at Starborough since at least the 14th century. Reginald, the first Lord Cobham, also owned nearby Hever Castle. Hever is a stunning place, better known as the childhood home of Anne Boleyn, and it's well worth visiting while you're in the area. Anyway, Lord Cobham held office as Admiral of the Fleet and Lord Warden of the Cinque Ports, and he took part in most of the battles in France and Flanders during the middle years of the 14th century. He fought at Crecy with the Black Prince, and was amongst the first of the Knights of the Garter.

Ironically, Lord Cobham survived his distinguished military career – and then died of the plague in 1361. In his will, the great man left Haxted Mill to his wife, Joan. It was a more enduring legacy than the family home because, in a further twist of fate, Parliament ordered the demolition of Starborough Castle at the end of the English Civil War. By contrast, the mill that you'll see on this walk still stands on the original foundations at Haxted.

It's an open question how long the first mill building survived. According to local tradition, Haxted Mill was founded by Richard III in the 15th century, though the earlier half of the present building was constructed on 14th-century foundations in around 1580. Perhaps the valley was well-wooded in those days for, as you'll see, the builders used hand-axed oak. You should be able to spot the smoother finish of the sawn pitch pine extension, which was added in 1794.

Haxted Mill carried on grinding flour until just after the First World War, when it switched to producing meal for the local farmers. Milling finally ended in 1945, and the building was opened as a museum in 1969. The present owners, Linda and David Peek, have only recently completed a comprehensive refurbishment.

After seeing the mill, you might want to drop in on Lord Cobham and his relations. His tomb is amongst several family memorials in Lingfield church, and his effigy lies in full plate armour, his head resting on a Moorish helmet. Look out for Cobham's own shield decorating the side of his tomb, together with those of his wife and several of his fellow Knights of the Garter.

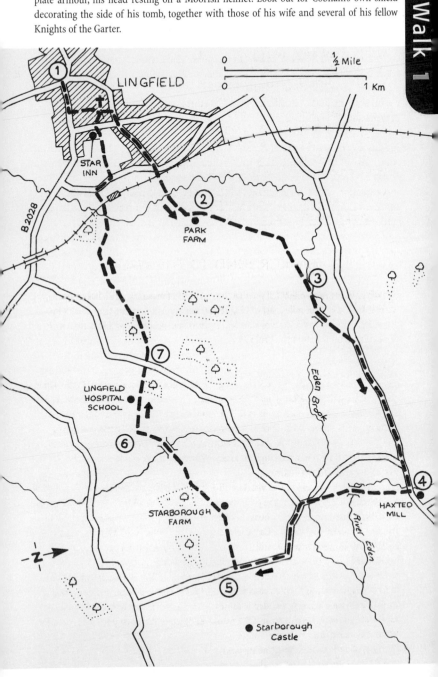

Walk 1

Walk 1 Directions

① Walk down **High Street**, turn left into **Old School Place**, and take the footpath through the churchyard. Turn right into **Vicarage Road**, cross over into **Bakers Lane**, and continue beyond **Station Road** onto the footpath across the railway. Swing left as you approach **Park Farm**, then fork left onto a gravelled farm track.

② Continue over the stile into an open field. A few paces further on, dodge through the gate on your left, and continue with the hedge on your right. At the top corner of the field, turn right through the small gate, heading past the prominent oak tree towards the gates on the far side of the field.

WHERE TO EAT AND DRINK ⓘ

Haxted Mill itself has a rather upmarket bar and brasserie with a riverside terrace overlooking the Eden. It's not cheap but it would supply a very nice excuse for doing a good walk. In Lingfield the Star Inn is a large town centre pub with an olde worlde atmosphere, good real ales and a selection of basket meals served all day. Children are welcome up to 9PM and dogs are welcome in the bar.

---

③ Cross the lane, climb over the stile opposite, and take the waymarked route beside the **Eden Brook**. Cross the brook on a wooden bridge, then head across the field to a stile by the metal gates. Turn right along the road to **Haxted Mill**.

④ Turn right over the stile onto the **Vanguard Way**, re-cross the river, and bear left towards the stile on the far side of the next field. Turn left onto the road, then fork left just beyond the bridge.

⑤ Turn right, along the drive towards **Starborough Farm**. At the farm, take the stile by the metal gates, cross the drive to **Badger House**, and follow the waymarked path across the field towards the corner of a small wood. Cross the footbridge and stile, and follow the path along the left hand edge of the next four fields.

⑥ Turn right in the corner of the fourth field, keeping the hedge on your left, and continue over a bridge and stile into **Lingfield Hospital Schoo**l sports ground. Keep straight on to a gap in the far hedge, then cross the lane, where the footpath continues at a stile.

⑦ Cross two small fields, enter the woods by the stile, and pass the children's adventure playground. Beyond the woods, bear right through the gates near the school buildings, and follow the winding path through the fields to the railway crossing near **Lingfield Station**. Turn right up **Station Road**; then, just opposite the station itself, turn left up a path to the **Star Inn**. Cross over **Church Road**, and turn right through the charming 16th-century **Old Town** into the churchyard. Finally, retrace your steps to the car park.

WHILE YOU'RE THERE ⓘ

Call into Haxted Water Mill which has been lovingly restored and has displays of milling equipment and the mill's history. If you've got a bit more time to spare, Hever Castle is not far away. Famed as a stunning, moated Tudor mansion, the site can trace its origins back to 1270 and was comprehensively restored and extended by William Waldorf Astor in 1903. It's quite expensive to get in but there is an adventure playground for children, two restaurants, gift, book and garden shops.

Oxted's Railway Intellectuals

Climb the North Downs escarpment and see how the coming of the railway changed village life in Oxted.

•DISTANCE•	5½ miles (9km)
•MINIMUM TIME•	3hrs
•ASCENT / GRADIENT•	607ft (185m) ▲▲▲
•LEVEL OF DIFFICULTY•	🚶🚶🚶
•PATHS•	Field edge paths, farm tracks, town roads, 12 stiles
•LANDSCAPE•	Dramatic chalk downlands and flatter, pastoral scenery
•SUGGESTED MAP•	aqua3 OS Explorer 146 Dorking, Box Hill & Reigate
•START / FINISH•	Grid reference: TQ 395529
•DOG FRIENDLINESS•	Good on Downs, around Oxted dogs must be on leads
•PARKING•	Ellice Road car park, off Station Road East, Oxted
•PUBLIC TOILETS•	At car park

BACKGROUND TO THE WALK

If Swindon or Crewe is your idea of a railway town, then you're in for a surprise. The railway came late to the medieval village of Oxted – just how late, we'll see in a moment – but it didn't destroy the character of the place. Instead, when Oxted expanded to embrace the new arrival, it developed its own unique style.

Couldn't Get a Railway

To begin with, it looked as though Oxted wouldn't get a railway at all. Parliament had authorised an independent line between Croydon and Royal Tunbridge Wells in 1865 but, in all but name, it was part of a turf war between two powerful companies competing for traffic between London and Hastings. Parts of the line were actually built, including the tunnel that you'll see on the walk. But there were all kinds of difficulties, including a riot against the contractor's Belgian workforce, and work was abandoned around 1870.

Years passed and, in 1878, Parliament approved new proposals for a railway linking Croydon, Oxted and East Grinstead. This time, the old rivals were working in partnership. The new scheme took over the abandoned works from the 1860s, and construction went ahead smoothly. After a wait of almost 20 years, the line through Oxted finally opened in March, 1884.

Didn't All Catch the Train

By coincidence, the Fabian Society of socialist thinkers was formed in the same year. One of its founder members was Edward Pease, who lived at nearby Limpsfield. He and others soon discovered that they could now live in a house in the country without having to cut themselves off from London society. Intellectuals such as DH Lawrence, George Bernard Shaw and Sidney and Beatrice Webb were amongst many who used the railway to attend Fabian gatherings in the area. The author Hilaire Belloc also used the railway – though he didn't come by train. In his book *The Old Road*, Belloc describes how he set out to prove the route of the Pilgrim's Way by walking the track from Winchester to Canterbury himself. He reached the cutting near Oxted tunnel at nightfall, and stumbled down the railway line in search of an inn.

As the area's popularity grew, the railway became the natural focus for expansion. From the dawn of the 20th century, right through to the 1930s, the Williams family of local builders developed the 'Oxted Mock Tudor' style to blend the new town with the half-timbered Tudor buildings of Old Oxted. The National Westminster Bank in Station Road East is a good example, but my own favourite is the Plaza cinema in Station Road West, built in 1930. You'll pass them both, near the start and finish of the walk, and you can compare them with the real thing on your way up through Old Oxted.

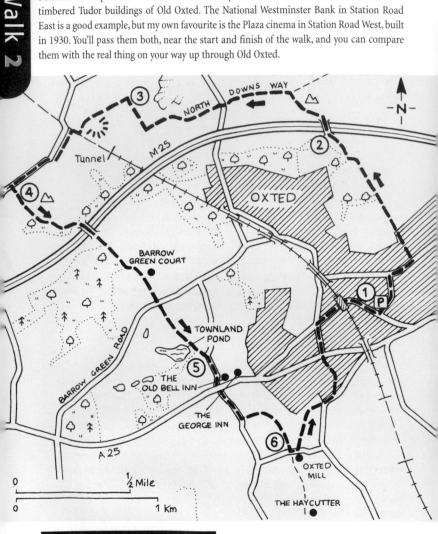

Walk 2 Directions

① Walk down **Station Road East** from the Ellice Road car park in Oxted. Turn left when you get to **Gresham Road**, then turn right at the top into **Bluehouse Lane**. Lastly, turn left again into **Park Road** and, at the bend, continue up the signposted public footpath towards **Woldingham**. Cross the stile beyond the school playing fields, and head across the field towards the footbridge over the intrusively noisy **M25 motorway**.

WHERE TO EAT AND DRINK ⓘ

On the High Street in Old Oxted, the **Old Bell** is a standard carvery-style pub with a heavily beamed Tudor interior. They also serve meals in a bar area where dogs are welcome. Nearby and also on the High Street is the **George Inn**, a relaxed and genteel pub with old beams, an excellent selection of real ales and a wide range of bar food. In Broadham Green the **Haycutter** is an unpretentious country pub, popular with locals. The food is traditional and worth waiting for. There's a garden and they serve mainstream real ales.

② Cross the motorway, bear left, and follow the path to the stile. Nip over, and swing left onto the **North Downs Way National Trail**. Follow the waymarked trail across **Chalkpit Lane** and past the quarry fencing, until it swings to the right for the assault on the North Downs ridge. Climb as far as the waymark post beyond the wicket gate, and bear left into the National Trust's **Oxted Downs** estate.

③ Follow the path as it burrows through the trees, cross the stile, and turn hard right up a flight of rustic steps. Don't miss the view from the seat halfway up, directly above the railway tunnel. Swing left at the top of the steps, and follow the National Trail to the road at **Ganger's Hill**.

④ Turn left, and drop back down the public footpath towards **Oxted**. Join the bridleway half-way down, and carry on across the bridge over the M25 onto the lane past **Barrow Green Court**. Cross over **Barrow Green Road**, squeeze through the wicket gate, then follow the footpath along the edge of the field past **Townland Pond** and out onto **Sandy Lane**.

⑤ Turn right, pass underneath the A25, and cross **Oxted High Street** at the Old Bell Inn. Follow **Beadles Lane** for 200yds (183m), then turn left into Springfield and fork off onto a footpath on the right. Drop gently down to **Spring Lane**, and the picturesque **Oxted Mill** (privately owned).

⑥ A 500yd (457m) diversion leads you to the **Haycutter** pub. Cross straight over **Spring Lane**, zig-zag right and left, then take the waymarked path through the meadows to the pub. The main route turns left past the mill, and left again over the stile at the weir. Follow the path through to **Woodhurst Lane**, and turn left. Fork left up the narrow footpath at **Woodhurst Park**, and cross the A25 into **East Hill Road**. At the foot of the hill, turn right up **Station Road West**, then dive through the station subway at the top. Finally, turn right into **Station Road East** to return to the start of your walk.

WHILE YOU'RE THERE ⓘ

The big draw in the area is undoubtedly Winston Churchill's home at **Chartwell**, to the south of Westerham. This country house, set in delightful gardens, is strongly evocative of the wartime leader and contains many mementos of his illustrious career. Owned by the National Trust there is the usual tea room and gift shop as well as excellent facilities for children.

The Outwood Miller's Trail

England's oldest working windmill marks the start of this secluded walk.

•DISTANCE•	6¾ miles (11km)
•MINIMUM TIME•	3hrs 30min
•ASCENT / GRADIENT•	328ft (100m) ▲▲ ▲
•LEVEL OF DIFFICULTY•	秋秋 秋秋 秋秋
•PATHS•	Easy field edge paths and farm tracks, 20 stiles
•LANDSCAPE•	Rolling farmland dotted with small patches of woodland
•SUGGESTED MAP•	aqua3 OS Explorer 146 Dorking, Box Hill & Reigate
•START / FINISH•	Grid reference: TQ 326456
•DOG FRIENDLINESS•	Can run free but keep on lead near livestock
•PARKING•	National Trust car park opposite mill, Outwood
•PUBLIC TOILETS•	None on route

BACKGROUND TO THE WALK

England was in the grip of the plague when Thomas Budgen of Nutfield built his mill on Outwood Common in 1665. And, according to tradition, the top of the newly-completed mill was just the spot to watch the Great Fire sweeping through London the following year.

A View to a Mill

Perhaps there was a similar view when Joseph Paxton's Crystal Palace burnt down in 1936; at any rate, you should be able to pick out the Crystal Palace television transmitter if the mill is facing north on the day that you go. Looking towards the mill, you'll find that it's screened from the surrounding lowlands by the nearby trees; you can see it best from Gayhouse Lane, and from the tracks at the start and finish of the walk.

Like any other mill, Outwood's sails will only turn when they are facing into the wind. So the 'post' mill is built around a huge vertical axle – or post – that allows the whole colossal structure to pivot as required. You'll see the oak post, reputedly brought from Crabbet Park, near Crawley, supported by a wooden framework resting on the four brick piers in the roundhouse. The body of the mill is almost 40ft (12m) high, and weighs around 25 tons, yet it's so well balanced that one person can turn it into the wind by pushing on the 'tailpole' at the back. The miller raises sacks of grain to the top with a hoist, powered by the sails, and feeds the grain down to the millstones on the floor below. The milled flour is then channelled to the spout floor at the bottom of the mill. Outside, the great wooden sails are built from slats resembling a Venetian blind. This system was first patented many years after Outwood mill was built, and must have replaced the original canvas sails.

For all its grandeur, Thomas Budgen's masterpiece wasn't the only mill on this site. A new smock mill was built just yards away in 1790, following a family quarrel. With its four pairs of millstones and other modern equipment, it was designed to drive the old-fashioned post mill out of business. But the new miller was rather too fond of the nearby Bell Inn and, when ill-fortune eventually led to the failure of his enterprise, the old post mill still soldiered on. The smock mill suffered the final indignity when it blew down during a storm in 1960. There's nothing left of it now, but you can still see the indentation where it stood, just behind the bungalow in the post mill grounds.

Walk 3

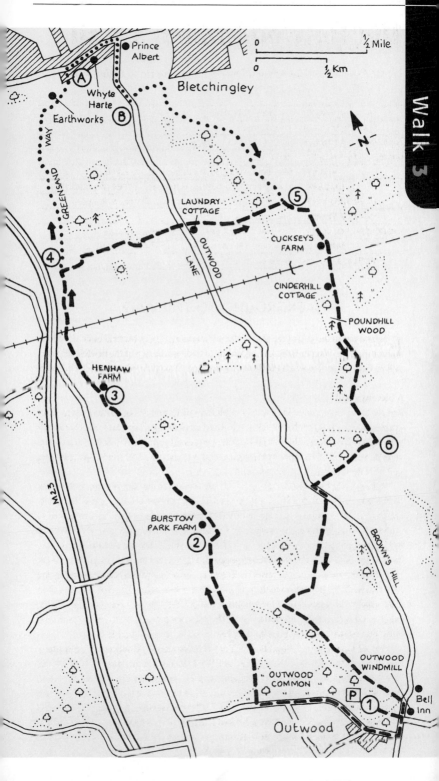

Prince Albert

Whyte Harte

Earthworks

Bletchingley

GREENSAND WAY

LAUNDRY COTTAGE

OUTWOOD LANE

CUCKSEYS FARM

CINDERHILL COTTAGE

POUNDHILL WOOD

HENHAW FARM

BURSTOW PARK FARM

BROWN'S HILL

OUTWOOD COMMON

OUTWOOD WINDMILL

Bell Inn

Outwood

M23

½ Mile

½ Km

N

Walk 3 Directions

① Head out of the car park towards the mill and keep turning right, via **Millers Lane** into **Brickfield Road**. Turn right down the woodland bridleway 180yds (165m) beyond the church, and follow it out into the fields towards **Burstow Park Farm**.

② Zig-zag right, then left, around the farmhouse to a metal gate. Jump the stile on your left, and walk diagonally across the field. Cross another stile, turn left through a gap in the hedge, then turn right towards the stile and footbridge at the top of the next field. Nip across, and bear left for 80yds (73m) to another stile and bridge. Bear left again over a stile, then turn right towards **Henhaw Farm**, where a stile leads up between the farm buildings.

WHERE TO EAT AND DRINK ⓘ

Sporting a 300-year old bell cast from a ships cannon, the **Bell Inn** on Outwood Lane in Outwood was once a coaching inn and is now a popular country pub/eaterie with log fires in its inglenook fireplace in winter. Children and dogs are welcome and there's a good selection of real ales and home-cooked bar meals. As well as a restaurant the Bell has a pleasant garden and a no-smoking area.

---

③ Cross the farm drive, and continue through a couple of fields before crossing the railway embankment via steep wooden steps and a level crossing. Now follow the fences on your left through three fields, as far as a metal field gate and stile.

④ Turn right here, but without crossing the stile. Follow the footpath through several fields, separated by stiles, always keeping the field edge on your left. Cross **Outwood Lane**, walk up the gravelled drive to **Laundry Cottage**, and take the narrow public bridleway just to the right of a metal field gate.

⑤ Pass a blue and yellow waymarker post, and continue along this easy-to-follow gravelled bridleway to **Cuckseys Farm** and **Cinderhill Cottage**. Now follow the waymarked route down beside **Poundhill Wood**, and carry on for another ¾ mile (1.2km) before emerging at the corner of an open field that rises gently to cut off the view.

⑥ Turn right here, along the woodland edge and onto the track leading out to **Brown's Hill**. Turn left, then right over the stile opposite **Outwood Swan Sanctuary**, and head diagonally across three fields. Bear gently right through a gap in the hedge, and continue through one field and into the next. After 40yds (37m) turn left over the waymarked stile and follow the field boundary on your left, past the National Trust waymarker post and into the woods on **Outwood Common**. Join the surfaced drive at Path End cottage, and follow it back to Outwood windmill and the start of your walk.

WHILE YOU'RE THERE ⓘ

You should really visit **Outwood Windmill** if you can. It's the oldest working post mill in England and has a small museum as well as a shop selling flour and souvenirs. It's open from Easter to the end of October, on Sundays only between 2PM and 6PM, so time your walk accordingly. If you can't fit it in, tours at other times can be arranged by appointment.

Outwood and the Bletchingley Loop

Bletchingley's wide High Street, with its shops and pubs, makes the village an attractive destination.
See map and information panel for Walk 3

•DISTANCE•	8¼ miles (13.3km)
•MINIMUM TIME•	3hrs
•ASCENT / GRADIENT•	525ft (160m) ▲▲▲▲
•LEVEL OF DIFFICULTY•	🚶🚶 🚶🚶 🚶

Walk 4 Directions
(Walk 3 option)

An attractive additional loop to the Outwood Miller's Trail (Walk 3), can be made by crossing the fields to the little town of Bletchingley, with its castle remains and bustling High Street.

Leave Walk 3 at Point ④, and cross over the stile onto the **Greensand Way**. This waymarked route carries you all the way into **Bletchingley** through a traditional wood pasture, with sheep grazing peacefully amongst the trees.

Even the sometimes intrusive presence of the nearby motorway can't disguise the medieval appearance of this landscape, as you dive into a tunnel of low trees and begin to climb the old sunken way up towards **Castle Hill**. The **Greensand Way** curves around the very foot of the castle earthworks, built for the de Clare family but destroyed some time after the Battle of Lewes in 1264. Although the castle's moat still remains, it is on private land and not open to the public.

Quite suddenly, you emerge into **Castle Square**. Keep straight on for the last 100yds (91m), then turn right into **Bletchingley High Street**, Point Ⓐ. Walk down as far as the Prince Albert pub, and turn right into **Outwood Lane**. Just beyond the houses, Point Ⓑ, turn left onto a public bridleway that winds uphill through a sunken way. Turn right at the brow, and follow the **Greensand Way** across a disused concrete road to the BT manhole 100yds (91m) further on. Branch off to the right here, say farewell to the **Greensand Way**, and follow the footpath diagonally across an open field into **Gravelhill Wood.**

Beyond the wood, continue over the waymarked stile, then follow the left hand side of the next field. Just before the corner of this field, swing left over a stile and head towards the woods. Continue just inside the woodland edge, until you cross a small plank bridge and rejoin the **Miller's Trail** at Point ⑤.

There's an excellent bus service from Redhill to Bletchingley, so if you'd rather leave your car at home you could start this walk from the High Street in Bletchingley instead.

Walk 5

Woldingham's Academic Eden

A relatively easy walk taking you through the enchanting valley setting of Woldingham School.

•DISTANCE•	3½ miles (5.7km)
•MINIMUM TIME•	1hr 30min
•ASCENT / GRADIENT•	295ft (90m) ▲▲▲
•LEVEL OF DIFFICULTY•	👣 👣 👣
•PATHS•	Surfaced lanes, wooded paths and bridleway, can be muddy, 2 stiles
•LANDSCAPE•	Valley farmland sheltered by woods on upper slopes
•SUGGESTED MAP•	aqua3 OS Explorer 146 Dorking, Box Hill & Reigate
•START / FINISH•	Grid reference: TQ 359564
•DOG FRIENDLINESS•	Dogs will need to be on lead for most of route
•PARKING•	Woldingham Road, 100yds (91m) north of railway station in Woldingham
•PUBLIC TOILETS•	None on route

Walk 5 Directions

You should come to Woldingham by train – and, preferably, from the south. I challenge anyone to gaze across this breathtaking landscape from the London platform, and not experience an immediate urge to pull on their boots, vault the railway fence, and amble off down the valley with a spring in their step and whistling a happy tune.

It is the kind of place which, when escaping from the city, you feel could lead you to anywhere, and never want to go back. But vaulting railway fences is against the law, so I'd better tell you the legal way of doing things. Turn right out of the station into **Church Road**, and keep going onto the unmade lane beyond **Church Farm**. Just over ½ mile (800m) from the railway station, you'll come across the

'**Woldingham Countryside Walk**' signpost which points your way over a stile on the right.

You'll find yourself on a narrow path, high above the railway cutting. After another 55yds (50m), turn hard right over the mouth of Woldingham tunnel to reach a second stile; nip over, and turn left along the waymarked path as it burrows through the trees and climbs steadily towards **Great Church Wood**.

Most of this area was considered to be a barren waste until 1672, when

> **WHERE TO EAT AND DRINK** ⓘ
> **Knight's Garden Centre**, passed on Woldingham Road at the end of the walk, has an attractive Conservatory Coffee Shop in landscaped grounds. It's unlicensed but does good light lunches, sandwiches and cakes. They tolerate dogs in their terrace garden

> **WHILE YOU'RE THERE** ⓘ
>
> **Godstone Vineyards** on Quarry Road, Godstone, just 400yds (366m) from Junction 6 on the M25, covers 50 acres (20ha) of Surrey farmland. There is a Vineyard Trail (free entry to individuals and families), a wine shop, tasting bar and garden room coffee shop. It's open all year round and welcomes children but not dogs.

Sir Robert Clayton, who later became Lord Mayor of London, bought the estate from a relative of the diarist John Evelyn. Sir Robert built the elegant Marden Park house and spent time and money laying out the grounds, so that when Evelyn visited him five years later, he was 'much pleased' by the walled gardens, the incredible solitude, and the innumerable plantations of young trees which had transformed the landscape.

It's nice to speculate that both men would enjoy the enduring peace of the 21st-century landscape. Great Church Wood is now owned by the Woodland Trust, and teeming with all kinds of wildlife; go quietly, and you may see tawny owls, roe deer, and woodpeckers. In springtime, the woodland floor is awash with bluebells and wood anemones, and the area is particularly known for its rare Roman snails.

At the top of the hill, turn right at the three-way wooden signpost and join the bridleway towards **South Lodge**. Turn left at the metal gate near the foot of the hill, still signposted to **South Lodge**, and drop down to the neat little graveyard on the left hand side. Turn right for the 70yds (64m) to **Marden Lodge**, then right again, and follow the bridleway drive through the parkland campus of Woldingham School.

Woldingham is part of a world-wide network of Catholic schools owned by the Society of the Sacred Heart, and was established here immediately after the Second World War. The school has grown steadily since that time, and you'll see the results of substantial new investment in recent years. Berwick House, designed to prepare senior girls for university life, opened in 1992 and, beyond the red brick mansion that replaced Sir Robert Clayton's house in 1879, lies the impressive new Millennium Performing Arts Centre. On your left, towards the end of the campus, comes the sports centre and, finally, Middle Lodge.

Now the drive follows the valley floor through glorious open farmland, framed by woodlands like jewels in a velvet box. Pass the turning to **Marden Park Farm**, and keep left at the white lodge cottage. Stay with the drive as it zig-zags under the railway; then, after 300yds (274m), turn right at the wooden public bridleway sign. Follow the grassy track as it winds around the edge of a small wood and meets the **Woldingham Road**. Cross over, turn right, and walk up past **Knight's Garden Centre** back to the railway station.

Walk 6

The Six Wives of Crowhurst

A lovely circular route on the trail of Henry VIII – and another man's wives!

•DISTANCE•	5 miles (8km)
•MINIMUM TIME•	2hrs
•ASCENT / GRADIENT•	131ft (40m) ▲ ▲ ▲
•LEVEL OF DIFFICULTY•	🚶 🚶 🚶
•PATHS•	Farm tracks and well-maintained field paths, some road walking, 10 stiles
•LANDSCAPE•	Gentle, well-farmed landscape
•SUGGESTED MAP•	aqua3 OS Explorer 146 Dorking, Box Hill & Reigate
•START / FINISH•	Grid reference: TQ 365453
•DOG FRIENDLINESS•	Will need to be on lead along roads, through farmyards, and near livestock. Large dogs may have difficulty with stiles
•PARKING•	Adjoining cricket field or in Tandridge Lane, Crowhurst
•PUBLIC TOILETS•	None on route

BACKGROUND TO THE WALK

What a gloriously remote part of Surrey this is! That assertion may strike you as somewhat improbable when you leave your car near the traffic lights, just a stone's throw from the busy A22. But trust me; a few hundred yards (metres) of road walking is a small price to pay for your admission ticket to this little-known corner of the county.

Courting Anne Boleyn

Nowadays, Crowhurst is on the way to nowhere at all, but apparently things were different in the 16th century. According to tradition, Henry VIII would stop over at Crowhurst Place on his way to court Anne Boleyn, who was living just over the Kentish border at Hever Castle. Even then, Crowhurst Place was not new. The lovely timbered and moated manor may be a spectacular example of what most of us loosely call 'Tudor', but it was already half a century old when that dynasty was ushered in on Bosworth Field in 1485.

Enough of the foreplay – you'll want to know about all those wives! The Gaynesford family first pop up during Edward III's reign, when John and Margery Gaynesford received the Manor of Crowhurst from the de Stangrave family. But it was another John Gaynesford – the Sheriff of Surrey, no less – whose dogged pursuit of an heir was to bring him an unbroken run of 15 daughters from his first five wives. His persistence was eventually rewarded when, at long last, he managed to father a son by his sixth wife.

The Gaynesford (later Gainsford) family lasted some 300 years at Crowhurst Place, and it's worth the short diversion to see their tombs, flanking the chancel of Crowhurst's little medieval church. There's also a 15th-century brass likeness of the John Gaynesford who was Surrey's Parliamentary representative in 1431.

Flagging in the Mud

Two hundred years later, one of John's descendants left an altogether different memorial of his own. We know from the 17th-century parish register that, in those days, it was 'a loathsom durtie way every steppe' from Crowhurst Place to the church. Tiring of these muddy pilgrimages, yet another John Gainsford paid £50 to have a stone-flagged causeway laid along the entire route. He got his money's worth, for the causeway still exists in places.

By the dawn of the 20th century Crowhurst Place was bearded with brambles, lonely and unloved. Its saviour was George Crawley, whose comprehensive restoration in 1920 even extended to the brand new mock-Tudor gatehouse on Crowhurst Road. Crowhurst Place isn't open to the public, but you'll see Crawley's handiwork clearly enough from the path, which runs within 100yds (91m) of the house.

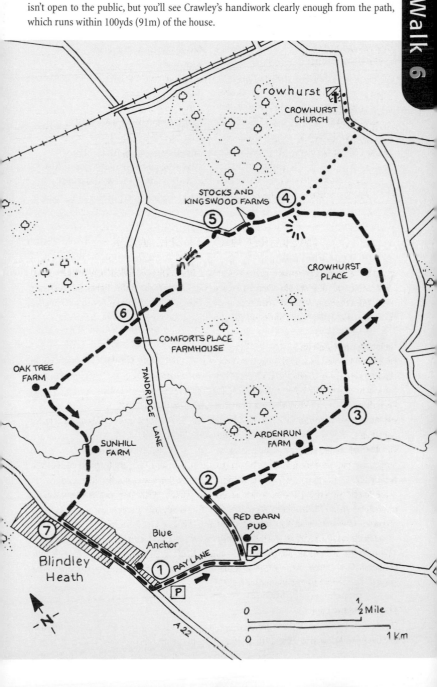

Walk 6 Directions

① Turn right out of the car park, and follow **Ray Lane** as far as **Tandridge Lane**. Turn left, pass the **Red Barn** pub, then turn right up the tree lined drive towards **Ardenrun**.

② Walk up the long straight drive until it swings to the left. Follow it for a further 80yds (73m) then, just before the private drive to **Ardenrun Farm**, swing hard right at the yellow waymark onto the 'Age to Age' walk. Continue for another 300yds (274m).

③ Nip over the stile on the left and walk through two gently rising fields. Turn right at the yellow 'Age to Age' waymark – where there are good views behind you - and follow the well-maintained path straight across the drive to **Crowhurst Place**. Continue beside the hedge on your right, cross a small footbridge, then head diagonally across the next field to the junction of two farm tracks. There are more good views from this spot and, if you want to visit **Crowhurst church**, you should turn right for 700yds (640m), then left onto **Crowhurst Road**.

④ Turn half left here, and follow the track towards **Stocks and Kingswood Farms**. Leave the 'Age to Age' route, and carry straight along the yellow waymarked track that winds through **Kingswood** farmyard, through a small wooden gate, and along the gravelled drive to the picture-postcard **Stocks Farm house**.

⑤ The gravelled drive joins a surfaced lane at the farm gate; turn left here and, after 20yds (18m), turn left again, over two stiles in quick succession. Head diagonally across the next field, and turn left over the stile. Cross a bridge and a second stile, then keep left until you cross another stile and a small footbridge. Now turn right, walk through two fields, and rejoin **Tandridge Lane**.

⑥ Turn left and, after 55yds (50m), branch off to the right at the entrance to **Comforts Place Farmhouse**. As the drive swings round to the left, nip over the stile and continue along the grassy lane to the rural crossroads at **Oak Tree Farm**. Turn left here, and follow the unmade track past **Highfield House** and out onto a muddy lane. Beyond **Sunhill Farm** the road surface improves, and the lane leads you back to the busy A22.

⑦ Turn left, and follow the main road for the last 800yds (732m) into **Blindley Heath** and back to the car park.

WHERE TO EAT AND DRINK ⓘ

You won't go hungry in Blindley Heath, which boasts two pubs offering extensive all-day menus. Despite its situation next to a filling station on the busy A22, the low, weatherboarded **Blue Anchor** is set well back from the road in its own gardens. With quarry tiled floors and winter log fires, it still retains some of the charm of a genuine country pub. By contrast, the busy family atmosphere of the **Red Barn** in Tandridge Lane rather offsets its quieter situation. But it's horses for courses, and this popular Brewer's Fayre outlet offers a large garden with a nice children's play area.

Around Gilbert Scott's Godstone

A relaxing walk through pleasant countryside, with something to interest the whole family.

•DISTANCE•	3¾ miles (6km)
•MINIMUM TIME•	1hr 45min
•ASCENT / GRADIENT•	278ft (85m) ▲▲ ▲▲ ▲
•LEVEL OF DIFFICULTY•	🚶 🚶 🚶
•PATHS•	Footpaths and bridleways can be muddy in places, 4 stiles
•LANDSCAPE•	Sheltered, domestic landscape dotted with little ponds
•SUGGESTED MAP•	aqua3 OS Explorer 146 Dorking, Box Hill & Reigate
•START / FINISH•	Grid reference: TQ 350515
•DOG FRIENDLINESS•	Please keep dogs on lead on village roads, through churchyard, and at Godstone Farm
•PARKING•	Adjacent to village pond. Parking limited to 3 hours, should be plenty for this walk
•PUBLIC TOILETS•	Outside Hare and Hounds pub

BACKGROUND TO THE WALK

It's no surprise to find that the two churches on this route were restored by Sir George Gilbert Scott. After all, Scott was one of the leading architects of the Victorian era; he headed the largest architectural practice of the time, and was associated with work on almost 500 churches.

Almhouses

Students of the great man need hardly come to Godstone, when they can see many of his largest and most famous buildings in London and other great cities. But, as you'll see, Godstone has one or two tricks up its sleeve. Sir George lived at Rook's Nest – now Streete Court School – less than a mile (1.6km) from the centre of the village; and, besides his work on the local churches, he also designed one of Godstone's most charming buildings.

You'll pass the low, mock-Tudor buildings of St Mary's Homes, right next to St Nicholas' Church. The almshouses were founded in 1872 by a young widow, Mrs Augusta Nona Hunt, for eight 'aged or infirm persons of good character'. With their profusion of little gabled windows, Sir George's designs seem almost to have grown out of the colourful, well-tended gardens that separate the Homes from Church Lane. A tiny chapel, heated by a fireplace in the west wall, completes this delightful group – do look in and see it, it's open to visitors daily. The Homes became a housing association in 1982, and are now a registered charity.

Philistine or Protector?

At about the time that he was building St Mary's Homes, Sir George was also involved in restoring St Nicholas' Church, and the Church of St Peter's in Tandridge. By now, some of his most famous projects – the Albert Memorial, the Home Office, and St Pancras Station in London – were already behind him. He had worked on many of the great cathedrals, too, but some people thought that his unusually thorough restorations destroyed too much of the original medieval work.

A letter that Scott wrote from Rook's Nest in 1871 suggests a different story. In it, he told fellow architect George Edmund Street how he was under pressure from an Oxfordshire rector to tear out the old pews from his church. Scott believed that the seating should stay; 'I value it no less for being humble', he wrote. 'It is good old work and in its place, and I hold that it is wrong to renew it... I wish especially that it shall not be renewed against my will or after I am away'. So – was Sir George really the philistine that he's sometimes made out to be, or a conservationist at heart? Pop into the churches on this route, and judge for yourself.

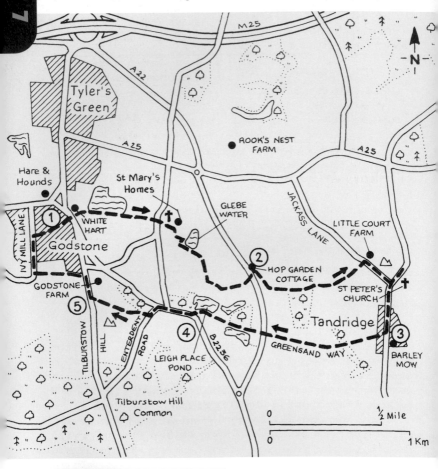

Walk 7 Directions

① Directly opposite the pond in Godstone, take the public footpath beside the **White Hart** pub, signposted towards the church. Cross **Church Lane** and follow the path through the churchyard.

Keep the church on your left, and continue along the winding path as it passes **Glebe Water** to a yellow waymarker post at the edge of an open field. Turn right and drop down beside the field to a stile, then turn left here onto the bridleway that leads under the busy A22.

Walk 7

② A few paces beyond the bridge, turn right at **Hop Garden Cottage** and follow the waymarked bridleway out onto **Jackass Lane**. Turn right here, opposite **Little Court Farm**, now converted into private houses. At the top of the hill, turn left for 100yds (91m) if you'd like to visit **St Peter's Church**. Otherwise turn right, and follow **Tandridge Lane** to the public footpath just 30yds (27m) short of the **Barley Mow**.

③ Turn right onto the waymarked **Greensand Way**, and follow the broad, sandy track between open fields to the wicket gate beside the busy A22. Cross the main road on the level, and take the footpath directly opposite. Beyond a small wood, a three-way wooden signpost guides you onto the bridleway straight ahead. Jump the tiny ford (or use the footbridge) and walk up the lane past **Leigh Place** pond as far as the B2236.

④ Leave the **Greensand Way** here, and turn right. Follow the pavement until just beyond **Church Lane**, then fork left at the bus stop, up **Enterdent Road**. After 100yds (91m) turn right onto the public footpath into the woods. The waymarked path climbs, steeply in places, to a stile near the adventure playground on the edge of **Godstone Farm**. Follow the waymarked route through the farm grounds, to the stile just north of the car park.

⑤ Turn right onto **Tilburstow Hill** for 100yds (91m); then, just beyond the **Godstone Farm** delivery entrance, turn off left at the wooden footpath signpost. The path runs briefly through farmland on the edge of **Godstone** village, then leads out into **Ivy Mill Lane**. Turn right for the short climb back to the village green, then right again, back to the car park at the start of your walk.

Walk 8

Happy Valley and Chaldon's Lucky Escape

The aptly-named Happy Valley leads you through heavenly countryside – to a vision of hell!

•DISTANCE•	3 miles (5km)
•MINIMUM TIME•	1hr 30min
•ASCENT / GRADIENT•	246ft (75m)
•LEVEL OF DIFFICULTY•	
•PATHS•	Well maintained and signposted paths, 7 stiles
•LANDSCAPE•	Downland and flower-rich grassland on Greater London's doorstep, some sections of woodland and working farmland
•SUGGESTED MAP•	aqua3 OS Explorer 146 Dorking, Box Hill & Reigate
•START / FINISH•	Grid reference: TQ 301571
•DOG FRIENDLINESS•	Some short sections where dogs must be on lead, there may be grazing animals at times
•PARKING•	Car park on Farthing Downs, open dawn till dusk
•PUBLIC TOILETS•	Godstone

BACKGROUND TO THE WALK

Nearly everything about this walk is surprising. The map shows a small triangle of countryside, gripped between the fingers of London's suburban sprawl and cut short by the M25 motorway. Yet, as you leave the wide horizons of Farthing Downs and amble through the peaceful hay meadows of the Happy Valley towards Chaldon, you could be a hundred miles from the capital.

If the countryside was lucky to escape development, your destination is even more remarkable. Inside Chaldon Church, the earliest known English wall painting was rediscovered under a layer of whitewash some seven centuries after it was created. Your walk begins in a stunning area of chalk downland, right on the Surrey border. Ironically, it was the Corporation of London that saved Farthing Downs from the expansion of London itself. Long before the Green Belt, the Corporation began protecting open spaces around the capital, and has owned and managed Farthing Downs since 1883.

The Celts were growing crops on these downs by the time of Christ, but they quickly exhausted the thin soil and, by Saxon times, the area was being used for burials. When the winter sun shines low over the short grass, you should be able to make out some of the low banks marking the Celtic field boundaries, as well as the circular mounds covering the Saxon graves.

Whitewashed Mural

The graves in Chaldon churchyard are more recent, but the building itself also dates from Saxon times and was mentioned in the Charter of Frithwald in the year 727. So the church was already old by the close of the 12th century, when a travelling artist monk created its greatest treasure – the terracotta and cream mural of the Last Judgement that covers most of the west wall. Heaven and hell are divided by a horizontal layer of cloud. A ladder links the two scenes, and fortunate souls climb towards eternal bliss, whilst the damned tumble off into the flames below. You can read the full story of this grotesque and complex vision in a leaflet in the church, but the wonder is that the painting survives at all.

Sometime around the 17th century the mural was whitewashed over, and it was only rediscovered during the redecoration in 1869 thanks to a sharp-eyed parish priest. When the Revd Henry Shepherd spotted some traces of colour on the wall he stopped the work, and arranged for the painting to be cleaned and preserved by the Surrey Archaeological Society. The mural has recently been cleaned again, following a thorough overhaul of the church itself. Look closely, and you should be able to spot the tiny corner that was left untouched, just to show the improvement.

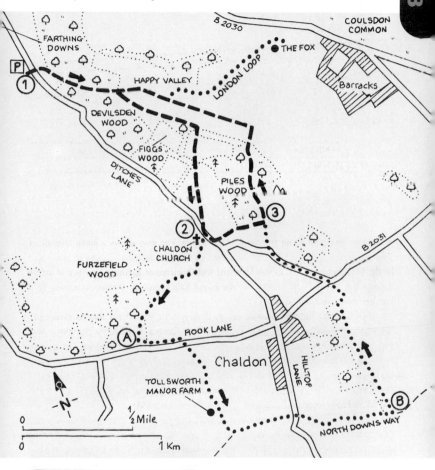

Walk 8 Directions

① Cross **Downs Road** from the car park, turn right at the information pagoda, and follow the waymarked **London Loop** down through **Devilsden Wood**. Beyond the woods, the **Happy Valley** opens up in front of you. Follow the woodland edge on your right until the path bears slightly left and begins to lose height. Now dodge briefly into the woods, and follow the signposted path towards **Chaldon Church**. Soon you'll be back in the open, and you follow the woodland edge as far as a wooden footpath sign. Turn right here, and walk through the thin finger of **Figgs Wood** before crossing a large open field.

WHAT TO LOOK FOR

You'll hear the continuous, liquid song of the **skylark**, long before you spot the scarcely visible speck that betrays its presence hundreds of feet above the grasslands of Farthing Down. But it's worth scanning the skies for this classic 'small brown job' because, after several minutes, you'll see it plummet to earth in a death-defying dive. Skylarks are ground nesting birds, and the female lays three or four eggs in a cup shaped grass nest that's often barely concealed. In winter, the resident population is boosted by large numbers of migrants from continental Europe.

WHILE YOU'RE THERE

There's always something new to see at Caterham's lively little **East Surrey Museum**, which regularly changes its displays of bygones from this corner of the county. Be prepared to encounter anything from local fossils and prehistoric flint tools to medieval pottery and Victoriana. There's also a room with special displays for children, with lots of things for them to see and touch. The museum is open on Wednesdays and Saturdays as well as Sunday afternoons, and has a gift shop, refreshments and toilets.

② At the far side of the field, turn left onto **Ditches Lane**; then, after 40yds (37m), fork right at the triangle to visit **Chaldon Church**. Return via the triangle to **Ditches Lane**, and continue for a few more paces in the direction you were going earlier. Now, you need to turn left onto the public footpath to **Piles Wood**. Cross the open field, and keep straight on when you come to the

WHERE TO EAT AND DRINK

The Fox is a large London 'country pub', with stone flagged floors and log fires in winter. It gets very busy but serves pretty good food from a menu of hot and cold bar fare. Families are welcome but dogs only in the garden. The tea room which used to be at the start of this walk, and is still shown on some maps, has now closed, but there is a small refreshment caravan selling tea, coffee snacks and ice creams most weekends and all week during the school summer holidays.

corner of **Piles Wood**. At the far side of the woods you'll come to a gravelled bridleway, where you turn left.

③ Follow the waymarked route of the **Downlands Circular Walk** as it drops down through **Piles Wood** to a footpath cross roads. Turn left, towards **Farthing Downs**, and continue for 700yds (640m) along the bottom of the **Happy Valley**. Should you feel thirsty, you can take the signposted route to **The Fox** that crosses the valley at this point. Turn right, and follow the London Loop waymarks to **Coulsdon Common**. The round trip to the pub will add a mile (1.6km) to your walk. Otherwise, continue for a further 70yds (64m), then fork left and climb gently up the side of the valley to rejoin your outward route at the corner of **Devilsden Wood**.

A North Downs Loop at Chaldon

The North Downs Way anchors this route to the national network, and there are some good views towards the Surrey border.
See map and information panel for Walk 8

•DISTANCE•	5½ miles (9km)
•MINIMUM TIME•	2hrs
•ASCENT / GRADIENT•	361ft (110m) ▲ ▲ ▲
•LEVEL OF DIFFICULTY•	🚶🚶 🚶🚶 🚶

Walk 9 Directions (Walk 8 option)

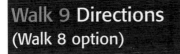

You can extend your walk in the Happy Valley by joining a section of the North Downs Way National Trail, a long-distance footpath extending from Farnham, all the way to Canterbury in Kent.

Follow Walk 8 as far as **Chaldon Church**. Pass the church and, as the road swings right to **Court Farm**, nip over the stile and take the path towards **Alderstead Heath**. The path crosses three fields then a stile into **Furzefield Wood**.

Fork left 20yds (18m) beyond the stile onto a concrete path, one of several that were built during the Second World War when this area was being used as a food store. Just before you get to **Rook Lane**, Point Ⓐ, turn left again onto the field edge path running parallel with the road, and follow it as far as the wicket gate on the right.

Follow the waymarked **Downlands Circular Walk** across **Rook Lane**, onto the concrete drive towards **Tollsworth Manor Farm**. Pass the pretty, rose-covered farmhouse; this was once the home of Patience Lambert, whose name appears on the pulpit at Chaldon Church and who now lies buried in the churchyard.

Stay with the **Downlands Circular Walk** as it dodges left and right off the concrete road, and follow it down the side of an open field. At the end of the field, the M23/M25 junction rises above the horizon at a gap in the hedge; turn left here, and join the **North Downs Way National Trail**. Cross **Hilltop Lane** and, after 750yds (686m), turn left off the **North Downs Way** onto the footpath signposted towards **Rook Lane**, Point Ⓑ.

Cross **Rook Lane** at the stile, and keep straight on into **Doctor's Lane**. Just past the pillar box, fork right into **Leazes Avenue**; then, 120yds (110m) further on, fork left at the little green, signposted towards the **Happy Valley**. A few paces further on, you rejoin Walk 8 at Point ③ to return to the car park on **Downs Road**.

Four Weddings and a Windmill

This linear walk along the Mole Valley follows the waymarked Greensand Way to Reigate Heath.

•DISTANCE•	3¾ miles (6km)
•MINIMUM TIME•	1hr 30min
•ASCENT / GRADIENT•	82ft (25m) ▲ ▲ ▲
•LEVEL OF DIFFICULTY•	🚶 🚶 🚶
•PATHS•	Rural paths, bridleways and village roads, 3 stiles
•LANDSCAPE•	Lowland landscape in Mole valley
•SUGGESTED MAP•	aqua3 OS Explorer 146 Dorking, Box Hill & Reigate
•START•	Grid reference: TQ 198494
•FINISH•	Grid reference: TQ 239503
•DOG FRIENDLINESS•	Take care at the village road crossings, and keep on lead across golf course
•PARKING•	Car park at Reigate Heath
•PUBLIC TOILETS•	None on route
•NOTE•	Catch bus 32 from car park to Brockham Green. Hourly service Monday–Saturday, 2-hourly on Sunday

Walk 10 Directions

Park your car at the finish and walk back to the A25, using the safe bridle track on the left-hand side of the road. Turn left to the bus stop, 40yds (37m) along the main road, and catch the number 32 bus to the start at **Brockham Green**.

Brockham is as charming a Surrey village as you could wish to find. The church, shop and two pubs cluster around the wide village green, whilst the River Mole flows placidly under the narrow bridges at the foot of the hill. It's generally a relatively peaceful place but can become surprisingly busy when, once a year, thousands of spectators gather for the village's spectacular annual Guy Fawkes bonfire and fireworks display.

WHILE YOU'RE THERE ⓘ
Seek out the recently restored post mill on Reigate Heath. It's on top of a small church, for which you can obtain the key from the nearby golf club's secretary's office, behind the clubhouse. It's free to enter this peculiar place at any reasonable time, but dogs are not allowed inside.

Get off the bus, walk across the village green to the **Dukes Head**, and turn right. After about 55yds (50m), bear left through a small white gate onto the **Greensand Way**, waymarked 'GW'. The narrow path leads you to a substantial footbridge over the **River Mole**; bear right here, onto a broad, tree-lined track. After 100yds (91m) look out for a heavily overgrown Second World War pill box nestling between the track and the river. There's a thoughtfully placed bench seat here too, and it's a very pleasant spot for a riverside picnic.

The track climbs gently to a three-way wooden signpost; keep straight on along the waymarked route towards **Betchworth**, then continue through St Michael's churchyard and up **Wonham Lane**, beside the **Dolphin** pub. But hang on! Isn't there something familiar here? St Michael's played a starring role as St John's Church, Stoke Clandon, in *Four Weddings and a Funeral*. Pop around to the lychgate on the north side of the church, and I think you'll recall seeing Charles and Scarlett (Hugh Grant and Charlotte Coleman) frantically changing their clothes after a last minute dash to Angus and Laura's wedding.

Back on the walk, the **Greensand Way** sidles off to the left just beyond the **Dolphin**, and follows the edge of an open field as far as **Sandy Lane**. Turn left, follow the road over a low hill to the T-junction opposite **Knowl Cottage**, and turn right. After 25yds (23m) turn right again, up a narrow flight of rustic steps to a stile. Nip across, follow the field edge to another stile, then turn left onto a **bridleway** for 150yds (137m). Now turn right over a 'GW' waymarked stile, and follow the

Greensand Way to **Dungates Lane**. Turn right, and continue past **Dungate's Farm** to the edge of **Reigate Heath golf course**. They've been playing golf here since 1895, so it's only fair to give golfers priority. Cross the course with care, then climb the heather-clad slopes of the low hill towards the clubhouse and **windmill**.

The windmill dates from around 1765, and is famous for the small church in its roundhouse. The mill is now anchored to face the prevailing wind; the sails no longer turn, and it isn't open to the public. But you can visit the church and take a look at the massive crosstrees and quarterbars that support the structure above.

Turn left onto the golf club drive, then, just past **Golf Cottage**, follow the **Greensand Way** down a grassy track on the right. Cross **Flanchford Road** and the golf course and keep **Bracken House** to your left as you follow the waymarked route up a woodland track. Pass **Tile House** and follow the path round to the **Skimmington Castle** pub. Turn left in front of the pub, then follow the waymarked route past the edge of the golf course and back to the car park at the beginning of the walk.

WHERE TO EAT AND DRINK   ⓘ

The **village shop** in Brockham sells pretty much everything you could ever need for a good picnic, but shuts at 3:30PM on a Sunday. Brockham Green has two pubs, both serving real ale and regular bar food. The **Royal Oak** is a cream-washed building on the village green with outside tables and a children's play area. Well-behaved dogs are also welcome. Nearby the **Duke's Head** is more of a local's pub and dogs are not allowed during food service hours. In Betchworth, head for the **Dolphin**, a 16th-century huddle of whitewash and tile hanging. It's a Young's house and serves a comprehensive menu of light snacks and bar meals. At Reigate Heath the **Skimmington Castle** restricts children to the garden but keeps dog biscuits behind the bar. Dating from 1485, the chimney was used as a lookout by highwaymen on the heath. Nowadays you'll find real ales and a good range of bar food from snacks to main meals.

The Battle for Banstead Commons

A popular, well-wooded route in the Chipstead valley.

•DISTANCE•	3½ miles (5.7km)
•MINIMUM TIME•	2hrs
•ASCENT / GRADIENT•	295ft (90m)
•LEVEL OF DIFFICULTY•	
•PATHS•	Woodland and field edge paths, muddy after rain, 7 stiles
•LANDSCAPE•	Wooded downland and working farmland
•SUGGESTED MAP•	aqua3 OS Explorer 146 Dorking, Box Hill & Reigate
•START / FINISH•	Grid reference: TQ 273583
•DOG FRIENDLINESS•	Can run free on Banstead Commons, although parts may be grazed. Keep on lead around Perrotts Farm
•PARKING•	Holly Lane, Banstead
•PUBLIC TOILETS•	At start

BACKGROUND TO THE WALK

The fight for London's countryside is nothing new, and the battle for Banstead Commons had all the ingredients of a good Victorian melodrama – an evil Baronet, who was defeated in the nick of time by the hand of fate.

Common Thief

Meet Sir John Hartopp MP, a Yorkshire Baronet. In 1873, Sir John bought the Lordship of the Manor of Banstead, together with a huge area of land that included the Banstead Commons. You'll be walking through Park Downs, a part of his holding, to the north of Holly Lane.

Most of the Commons were subject to grazing and other rights. This could have thwarted Sir John's plans for a housing development on Banstead Downs, and the sale of minerals from Banstead Heath. In practice, the rights were all but extinct, but Sir John began to consolidate his position by buying them up for himself.

Determined to see some return on his investment, Hartopp raised his game. In 1876 he built a row of houses on Banstead Downs, and enclosed a part of Banstead Heath. The locals were furious, and formed the Banstead Commons Protection Society. They enlisted the help of the newly formed Commons Society, as well as the Corporation of London and the area's largest landowner, the seventh Earl of Egmont.

Dragged Down by Insolvency

Battle was joined. In 1877 the protesters began court proceedings to challenge the enclosure of the heath, and a hugely expensive case dragged on until 1884. Just as a compromise seemed certain, fate intervened. Sir John's solicitors suddenly became insolvent, and Hartopp himself was dragged down with them. It strengthened the protesters' hand – but it delayed their ultimate victory until 1889.

Realising that the future was far from secure, the commoners went on to petition for an Act of Parliament to protect the Commons. The result was the appointment of the

Banstead Commons Conservators in 1893, and the Conservators continue to manage the Commons to this day.

But the countryside didn't always come out on top. When you cross over Holly Lane, you'll notice some mature houses on each side of the road. By coincidence, their story also begins in 1893, when Charles Garton bought the Banstead Wood Estate. He was destined to become Chairman of the Parish Council, and the last of the area's big, patriarchal landowners. When Charles Garton died in 1934, the land on each side of Holly Lane was sold for development, and Banstead Wood House itself formed the basis of a new hospital. As I write, you can still see the hospital's tower from Park Downs; but the 'For Sale' boards have gone up again, and the next chapter is waiting to be written.

Walk 11 Directions

① Leave the car park by the wicket gate at the top left-hand (south east) corner, and follow the waymarked gravel path. After 80yds (73m), join the public footpath

towards **Perrotts Farm**. The path climbs steadily through a tunnel of trees along the woodland edge. Look out for the old beeches on your right, nuzzling against one another and joined at the roots; these may once have formed part of an old boundary hedge.

Walk 11

② At the three-way wooden signpost ½ mile (800m) from the car park, you have the option of a diversion to the **Ramblers Rest**. Continue straight along the permissive path, signposted towards **Fames Rough**. Then, 200yds (183m) further on, bear right at another three-way signpost, towards **Banstead Wood**. Carry on through Fames Rough, turn left onto the **Banstead Countryside Walk** at the next three-way signpost, and follow it to a waymark, 220yds (201m) further on.

WHAT TO LOOK FOR ℹ

Go quietly along the woodland edges, and there's a good chance that you'll see an engaging little group of long tailed tits. Listen for their thin *tseep-tseep* calls as they bounce restlessly through the trees in their distinctive black, white and pink plumage. These tiny birds roam the woods feeding on small insects, and they're the only common British birds of their size with such a long tail. Despite being only 5½ inches (14cm) long – including a 3-inch (8cm) tail – they can travel as far as 25 miles (40.5km) in a single day.

---

③ Here the **Banstead Countryside Walk** dives off into the undergrowth on the left. Keep straight ahead, nipping over the fallen tree trunk a few paces further on. Soon the path narrows and bears to the right, and you leave **Fames Rough** by the stile at the corner of an open field. Follow the edge of the woods on your right, as far as the buildings of **Perrotts Farm**.

④ Jump the stile here, cross the farm road, and take the signposted footpath towards **Holly Lane**. Follow it along the left hand side of the field and over a stile, onto a gravelled farm track. Continue in

the same direction along the edge of **Ruffett Wood**, and carry on along the signposted path towards **Park Downs**. The path crosses the grandly named **Chipstead Road** – little more than a track, really – at a stile, before bearing right and meeting **Holly Lane**.

⑤ Cross **Holly Lane**, and nip over the stile opposite, still signposted towards **Park Downs**. Follow the hedgerow trees on your left until you come to the stile 50yds (46m) beyond the top corner of this field. Turn left over the stile, then bear left along the edge of **Park Downs**. Keep straight on at the four-way signpost, and follow the waymarked **Banstead Countryside Walk** back to the car park at the junction of **Park Road** and **Holly Lane**.

WHERE TO EAT AND DRINK ℹ

There's a simple refreshment hut at the start of the walk for teas and ice creams, but if you're hankering after something more substantial try the **Mint** on Park Road in Banstead, It's a welcoming old pub festooned with flower baskets in summer. The cosy stone-flagged bars have beamed ceilings and log fires, and there's real ale and a well-presented menu of hot and cold bar food. The **Rambler's Rest** in Chipstead will always be attractive to walkers. It is a large, sprawling half-timbered farmhouse complex with parts dating back to 1301. Dogs are welcome but it can get very busy at weekends.

Jumbos at Charlwood

An easy-to-follow route with something to interest everyone – especially plane spotters!

•**DISTANCE**•	4¼ miles (6.8km)
•**MINIMUM TIME**•	1hr 45min
•**ASCENT / GRADIENT**•	197ft (60m)
•**LEVEL OF DIFFICULTY**•	
•**PATHS**•	Byways and woodland paths, short sections on village roads and farmland, 7 stiles
•**LANDSCAPE**•	Well wooded, agricultural scenery
•**SUGGESTED MAP**•	aqua3 OS Explorer 146 Dorking, Box Hill & Reigate
•**START / FINISH**•	Grid reference: TQ 243410
•**DOG FRIENDLINESS**•	Keep on lead along roads and through Greenings Farm
•**PARKING**•	On The Street, close to Rising Sun and post office
•**PUBLIC TOILETS**•	None on route

BACKGROUND TO THE WALK

I'm most certainly not a plane spotter. But I will confess to a certain frisson of excitement every time I see a big jet dropping smoothly onto the tarmac, or climbing off the runway like a rocket. It's an awesome business – and that's before you consider the logistics of handling the passengers.

Close to the Border

Well, Gatwick airport may be in Sussex, but there's no escaping its impact on this corner of Surrey. So, rather than put sacks over our heads and ignore the area completely, I thought it might be fun to get a decent look at the place. You'll see plenty of aircraft on this walk, which passes within ½ mile (800m) of the end of the runway.

The airport may be a child of the 20th century, but the name goes back to 1241, when Richard de Warwick assigned the rights over 22 acres (8.9ha) of land in the Manor of Charlwood to one John de Gatwick. The land subsequently became part of the Manor of Gatwick, and remained in the same family until the 14th century. More recently, the Gatwick Race Course Company opened for business in 1891. The Aintree Grand National was abandoned during the latter years of the First World War, and a substitute race was run over the Gatwick course. Lester Piggott's grandfather, Ernie Piggott, was the 1918 winner, riding a horse called Poethlyn.

Cheap Fares

The Surrey Aero Club started flying at Gatwick in 1930, and the Air Ministry issued Gatwick's first commercial licence in 1934. Scheduled services began in May 1936; at that time a single fare to Paris cost just four pounds and five shillings (£4.25), and the price included the rail fare from London! The airport was requisitioned during the Second World War, and post-war operations resumed when the Queen opened London's new £7.8m airport in June 1958. Today, Gatwick is the busiest single runway airport in the world. The statistics are mind-numbing. Over 100 airlines carry more than 30 million passengers a year to some 280 destinations worldwide. On average, an aircraft lands or takes off every 2 minutes of every day in the year, and the airport generates employment for around 27,000 people. Even if you're not flying, you'll find the airport a total contrast to your walk in the woods. You can browse around a wide range of famous name stores, with prices the same as you'd pay in the high street. And there's plenty of choice when it comes to food and drink too; everything from an all-day breakfast in Garfunkel's, to a pint of real ale in a Wetherspoons pub.

Who knows? You might even indulge in a little plane spotting.

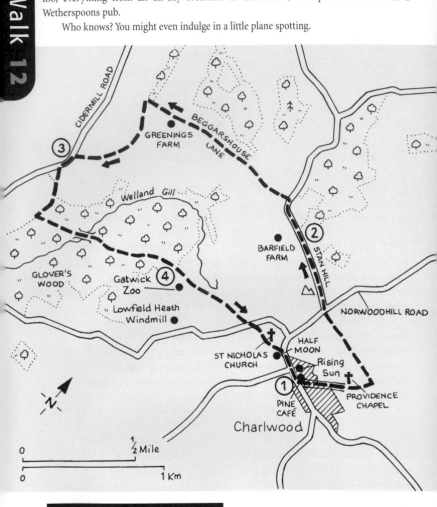

Walk 12 Directions

① With the recreation ground on your right, walk past the **Pine Café**, and turn left up **Chapel Road**. Continue onto the byway and pass the extraordinary **Providence Chapel**. Behind the low picket fence, a few tombstones lean

drunkenly in front of this small, weatherboarded chapel with its wooden verandah. The building, which dates from 1816, is straight out of an advert for Jack Daniels, and seems to have dropped in from Kentucky.

Turn left at the byway crossroads towards **Stan Hill**, and continue

Walk 12

WHAT TO LOOK FOR ⓘ

Look out for the sails of Lowfield Heath windmill. It was built about 1740, and used to grind flour until about 1880. It was moved here in 1987 when its site at Lowfield Heath was needed for expansion at Gatwick airport. Fully restored in 1999, visitors can walk around the outside of the mill, free of charge, at any reasonable time. The mill is normally fully open on the last Sunday of the month during the summer, but please ring to check before travelling.

straight across **Norwoodhill Road**. At the brow of the hill, take the signposted footpath on the left, just at the entrance to **Barfield Farm**.

② The path leads to the corner of **Beggarshouse Lane**, where you turn left, and follow the lane onto the tree-lined byway. At the woods beyond **Greenings Farm**, turn left over a plank bridge and waymarked stile. Follow the left-hand edge of an open field, then cross the farm lane at a pair of waymarked stiles. Continue over another pair of stiles until the fence bears left at a stile. Steer gently right here, towards the stile in the far corner of the field, then head across the next field to the stile into **Cidermill Road**.

③ Turn left, and follow the wide grass verge for 75yds (69m) before turning left again onto the signposted bridleway. Soon the path dodges into **Glover's Wood** and, 200yds (183m) further on, you'll come to a pair of waymarker posts. Turn hard left at the first one, follow the waymarked footpath across **Welland Gill**, and carry on to the far side of the woods.

④ Leave the woods at a wicket gate, and continue straight down **Glovers Road**. Cross **Rectory Lane/Russ Hill Road**, and keep straight on down the footpath opposite. The path passes **St Nicholas Church** – but you must not.

Inside this welcoming church are some of the finest medieval wall paintings in the country. Most poignant is a hunting scene, fairly common in artwork from around the time of the Black Death, in which three youths encounter three skeletons. 'As you are, we were' say the skeletons, before adding 'as we are, you will be...'

Beyond the churchyard, turn right past the **Half Moon**, then right again for the last 100yds (91m) back to the recreation ground.

WHILE YOU'RE THERE ⓘ

Zoos are not everyone's cup of tea, but **Gatwick Zoo** has made a niche for itself in its child-oriented, hands-on approach. They positively encourage close contact between the animals and visitors. There are over 10 acres (4ha) of landscaped grounds, enclosures and tropical houses, containing more than 1,000 small mammals, birds and seasonal butterflies from around the world.

WHERE TO EAT AND DRINK ⓘ

Try the **Pine Café** in Charlwood. It's a combination of pinewood showroom, post office and café and they serve reasonably-priced sandwiches and hot snacks. Also on The Street in Charlwood you'll find the **Half Moon**, an intimate, low-beamed village local tracing it's origins back to the 15th century. They serve real ales and large filled baguettes as well as bar meals. Dogs are welcome. Nearby, the **Rising Sun** looks a little forbidding from the front, but is comfortable and welcoming inside. They serve the usual pub favourites and hand pulled ales. Well behaved dogs on leads are tolerated.

Holmwood's Highway and its Men

Squatters and smugglers, highwaymen and a hero – Holmwood has them all!

•DISTANCE•	3¼ miles (5.5km)
•MINIMUM TIME•	1hr 15min
•ASCENT / GRADIENT•	164ft (50m) ▲▲▲
•LEVEL OF DIFFICULTY•	䍅 䍅 䍅
•PATHS•	Forest and farm tracks, muddy in places, some minor roads
•LANDSCAPE•	Wooded common, with clearings and scattered houses
•SUGGESTED MAP•	aqua3 OS Explorer 146 Dorking, Box Hill & Reigate
•START / FINISH•	Grid reference: TQ 183454
•DOG FRIENDLINESS•	Welcome on Holmwood Common, please remember to poop scoop, especially in car park area
•PARKING•	National Trust car park at Fourwents Pond
•PUBLIC TOILETS•	None on route

BACKGROUND TO THE WALK

Visit Holmwood today, and you'll find a peaceful tangle of woodland, bracken and grass, with several decent car parks and the placid Fourwents Pond glistening calmly in the south east corner of the common. Pretty much what you'd expect, really, from an area that's been in the hands of the National Trust since 1956. Nevertheless, the common has a rather more turbulent history than you might guess.

Holmwood was part of the Manor of Dorking and was held by King Harold until William took over at the time of the Norman conquest. Perhaps the area had little to interest the Conqueror; at that time Holmwood was something of a wasteland, and it didn't even get a mention in the Domesday Book.

Use It or Lose It

By the Middle Ages, squatters had begun to move in. They built makeshift houses, grazed a few animals, and cleared the woodland for timber and fuel. The new residents also went in for sheep stealing and smuggling, as well as the more honest trade of making brooms.

Smuggling remained rife well into the 18th century. Nearby Leith Hill tower was used for signalling during the 1770s, and the bootleggers also met in pubs and cottages on the common itself. One of these, the Old Nag's Head, once stood on the corner of Holmwood View Road and the A24 (Point Ⓓ on the map). Brook Lodge Farm, just up the road from Fourwents Pond, stands on the site of another smugglers' haunt; the old Bottle and Glass.

Just Passing Through

Meanwhile, efforts were being made to improve local communications, which had become rather worse than when the Romans drove the road which became Stane Street across the common on its way from London to Chichester. In 1755 a turnpike road was built on the line of the modern A24, and up to 18 coaches a day began rolling through Holmwood. As a result, highwaymen prospered here until well into the 19th century.

American Millionaire

But the new road had its fair share of gentlemen, too. The American millionaire Alfred Gwynne Vanderbilt regularly drove his coach along this stretch, and he made many English friends. He died tragically in May 1915, when the Cunard liner *Lusitania* was torpedoed by a German U-boat off the southern coast of Ireland. Gallant to the last, Vanderbilt is said to have helped search for children on the sinking ship, and gave his own lifebelt to an elderly lady passenger.

You can see Vanderbilt's simple granite memorial, erected on his favourite road by a few of his British coaching friends and admirers, by making a short diversion along the roadside pavement from South Holmwood and crossing near the bus shelter.

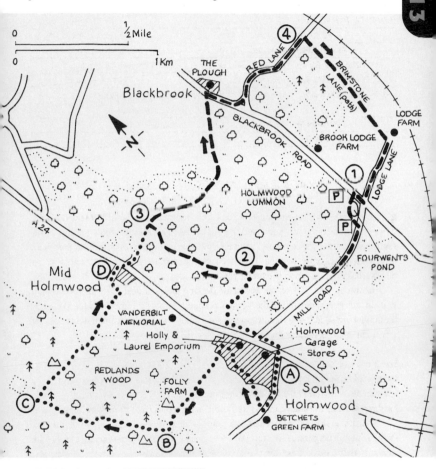

Walk 13 **Directions**

① Head out of the car park towards **Fourwents Pond**, and bear right along the waterside track, keeping the pond on your left. At the far corner of the pond, cross a small plank bridge, walk through the smaller car park, and turn right into **Mill Road**. After 400yds (366m), turn right up the lane signposted '**Gable End, Applegarth and Went Cottage**'; then, 30yds (27m) further on, fork left onto the waymarked public footpath.

Walk 13

Continue under a set of power lines, then follow the blue waymarks across the parting of two rough gravel tracks before re-crossing one of them at another blue waymark. Follow the path to the next waymarker post and swing left at the yellow arrow that points your way to **Clematis Cottage**. Turn right here, and join the gravelled track as far as **Uplands Cottage**.

> **WHAT TO LOOK FOR**
> In the summer months of June, July and August, watch out for **white admiral** butterflies feeding on bramble blossom in the woodland glades. Somewhat confusingly, the white admiral's wings are mainly charcoal grey, but with a broad white streak running from front to back down each side. The butterfly has a slow, measured flight and, although it sometimes congregates when feeding, you'll generally see them alone. Its green caterpillars feed only on sweet-smelling honeysuckle.

② Turn left for 20yds (18m), then slip away to the right onto a grassy footpath. At the end of the footpath turn right, dodge through a wooden post and rail barrier, then turn left at the blue and yellow waymarker post, 25yds (23m) further on. Fork right at the next junction of paths to a clearing in the woods and drop down the grassy slope straight ahead, now following the blue waymarked route onto a gravelled surface at the foot of the hill. After 300yds (274m), keep a sharp eye out for a blue and yellow waymarker to the left of the path, and turn right here, onto another gravelled path.

③ This yellow waymarked route leads purposefully across the **Common** beside the National Trust estate boundary, and brings you out opposite the **Plough** pub at

> **WHERE TO EAT AND DRINK**
> The whole family's welcome at the traditional **Plough** at Blackbrook, half-way around this route; you can even take the dog into the Blackbrook bar. You've a choice of three real ales, plus a good selection of competitively priced lunchtime bar snacks, salads and meals. If all you want is a quick bite on the hoof, pop into the **Holmwood Garage Stores** on the A24 at South Holmwood to stock up on chocolates, ice creams, soft drinks and snacks. For something a bit more substantial, head for the **Holly and Laurel Emporium** just up the road. Beyond the clutter of antiques you'll find an attractive tea room where you can get hot drinks, home made cakes, light lunches and cream teas.

Blackbrook. Turn right onto **Blackbrook Road**, then left into **Red Lane** (signposted towards **Leigh** and **Brockham**) and follow it for about ½ mile (800m).

④ Turn right into **Brimstone Lane** at the public bridleway signpost. Continue through a five-bar gate and down the right-hand side of an open field, leaving through a second

> **WHILE YOU'RE THERE**
> From Fourwents Pond, you're well placed to visit the **Dorking Museum**. Here you'll find collections of farm tools and equipment, clothing and household items, all with a local connection. There's a children's corner, and the collection of stuffed birds is popular with youngsters, too. Discover the story behind the Dorking cocks that feature in the Mole Valley coat of arms, and see the remains of Dorking's very own dinosaur – a 10ft (3m) iguanadon tail bone.

gate at the far end. Follow the track as far as **Lodge Farm**, then turn right onto **Lodge Lane**, which leads you back to the **Fourwents Pond**. Turn right here, for the last 100yds (91m) back to the start.

Redlands Wood Loop

Extend your time at Holmwood with this loop in quiet woodlands.
See map and information panel for Walk 13

•DISTANCE•	6 miles (9.7km)
•MINIMUM TIME•	2hrs 30min
•ASCENT / GRADIENT•	607ft (185m) ▲▲▲
•LEVEL OF DIFFICULTY•	🚶 🚶 🚶

Walk 14 Directions (Walk 13 option)

Leave Walk 13 at Point ②, and turn left onto a grassy track. After 300yds (274m) it swings to the right and comes to a crossroads. Turn left, and continue towards the busy A24 until the roadside houses come into view; then bear left, and walk parallel to the main road. Continue past **Mill Road** to the war memorial, then cross the main road via the subway, Point Ⓐ.

Now take the quiet lane up towards **Betchets Green Farm**. Fork right just beyond the farm, and turn sharp right at the public footpath sign 75yds (69m) further on. Follow the path over two stiles, bear left into **Warwick Close**, and continue until the road ends at a public bridleway. Turn left, walk past Folly Farm, and begin climbing towards **Redlands Wood**, Point Ⓑ.

After 450yds (411m) you'll come to a rough forest ride. Turn right, and continue up the hill until the ride swings left to a five-way junction. Think of it as a mini-roundabout, and take the third exit. You'll climb briefly, before dropping to a forest crossroads, Point Ⓒ.

Turn right, then right again at the blue waymark arrow. Keep straight ahead at the junction 130yds (119m) further on, now following the yellow waymarker. At the bottom of the hill swing right over a brook; then, almost at once, fork left onto a narrow footpath just inside the woodland edge. A stile leads you out of the woods and across an open field to another stile. Nip over this and continue following the track as it zig-zags left and right into **Norfolk Lane**, back to the A24, Point Ⓓ.

Cross the dual carriageway with care and walk down **Holmwood View Road**. Continue along the grassy footpath at the bottom to rejoin the main route at Point ③.

WHAT TO LOOK FOR ℹ️

You may just be lucky enough to spot one or two of the shy **roe deer** that live in Redlands Wood. At around 25in (65cm) at the shoulder, these graceful creatures are smaller than the more common **fallow deer**, which grow to around 3ft (90cm) tall. The young roe fawns have a dappled coat but, unlike fallow deer, the adults are never spotted; their coats are foxy red in summer, toning down to a dark grey-brown in winter. Look out, too, for their distinctive two-toed footprints or 'slots' in the muddier parts of the forest.

Walk 15

Cherkley's Famous Media Magnate

A walk in the woods around the former country home of one of the great press barons, Lord Beaverbrook.

•DISTANCE•	3 miles (4.8km)
•MINIMUM TIME•	1hr 30min
•ASCENT / GRADIENT•	410ft (125m)
•LEVEL OF DIFFICULTY•	
•PATHS•	Fenced, easy-to-follow tracks around estate boundary
•LANDSCAPE•	Wooded, with some views across surrounding valleys
•SUGGESTED MAP•	aqua3 OS Explorer 146 Dorking, Box Hill & Reigate
•START / FINISH•	Grid reference: TQ 193546
•DOG FRIENDLINESS•	Watch out for them running after rabbits or deer
•PARKING•	Mill Way, almost opposite Nower Wood Nature Reserve
•PUBLIC TOILETS•	None on route

Walk 15 Directions

Cherkley Court began life as a kind of granny-annexe, when the wealthy Midlands industrialist Abraham Dixon built the great house in the early 1870s as his retirement home. The Surrey countryside clearly suited him, for he lived at Cherkley until his death more than 30 years later.

Meanwhile, Cherkley's future was being played out on the far side of the Atlantic. After making his first fortune from the cement business, Canadian-born William Maxwell Aitken shut up shop and emigrated

to England in 1910. The next 12 months were a whirlwind; he was elected to Parliament, acquired a knighthood – and bought Cherkley Court.

The newly knighted Sir Max Aitken probably got his first glimpse of Cherkley from one of the main carriage drives, but we must approach this private estate from a different direction. Two bridleways diverge from the car park in **Mill Way**. Take the right hand fork, with the golf course on your right, and drop gently down through a tunnel of trees to cross **Stane Street** at a four-way signpost. Keep straight on, and cross the drive to C**herkley Court** at **Upper Lodge**. When I last saw the building it was a forlorn, bricked up cottage, but restoration plans are in the air.

The track narrows at the lodge, and continues down the hill for a further 800yds (732m). Just as the path sinks into a shallow cutting, a

> **WHERE TO EAT AND DRINK** ⓘ
> The **Cock Horse**, next to Headley church, has a traditional public bar in the original pub building. A more modern, food-orientated bar in a recent extension now forms the main entrance. It's up a steep flight of steps, but there's disabled parking and access in the upper car park.

Walk 15

footpath crosses your route. There's a waymarker post here; turn left, and climb gently past the houses and gardens backing onto the hedge on your right. As you crest the brow and begin to wind downhill, keep an eye out on the left for glimpses of **Cherkley Court**.

The outbreak of the First World War did little to halt Aitken's meteoric rise. He gained control of the *Daily Express*, and subsequently founded both the *Sunday Express* and the *London Evening Standard*. At the same time, he achieved considerable political influence. He was ennobled as Lord Beaverbrook in 1916, and served in the Cabinet during both World Wars.

Throughout this time Cherkley was the focus of Beaverbrook's media empire. The news streamed into his office on ticker tape, and he was deeply involved in the day to day running of his newspapers. But a great country house was also an indispensable political asset. Here, politicians could meet and manoeuvre; Beaverbrook entertained lavishly, regularly

welcoming famous names like Herbert Asquith, David Lloyd George and Winston Churchill.

Beyond **Cherkley Hill electricity sub station** the path drops more steeply, rounds a brick wall, and crosses another estate drive at **Lower Lodge**. Beyond the drive, climb the short flight of steep rustic steps that lead to a pleasant, gently rising path through a centuries-old thicket of yew trees.

> **WHILE YOU'RE THERE** ⓘ
> Inside the 17th-century, timber-framed Hampton cottage in Church Street, Leatherhead, you'll find **Leatherhead's Museum of Local History**. Besides its comprehensive displays of memorabilia, maps and old photographs, the museum also features a collection of Ashtead art deco pottery and figurines from between the two World Wars.

The path ends at a T-junction with **Stane Street**. Turn left at the three-way signpost, towards **Thirty Acres Barn**. Follow this ancient route uphill and down dale, until at length, it climbs to a cross roads, and the four-way signpost that you passed on your outward journey. Turn right towards **Mill Way**, and retrace your outward steps to the car park. You'll get a different perspective on the way back, with good views across the **Tyrrell's Wood** golf course to the clubhouse in the trees on the skyline.

> **WHAT TO LOOK FOR** ⓘ
> For part of this route you'll be walking along **Stane Street**, the great Roman highway from Chichester to London. History is only skin deep here; in recent times, local people have found Roman coins buried just below the surface of the track. The road was built during the 1st century AD, although its name – which simply means 'stone road' – dates only from Saxon times. You can follow Stane Street on foot for almost 3 miles (5km) between Juniper Hill and Thirty Acres Barn, and a similar stretch lies buried under the modern A29 at Ockley.

Lord Beaverbrook lived at Cherkley for over half a century, and died there in 1964. The Beaverbrook Foundation is now restoring the estate, with the long term aim of opening the house and grounds as his public memorial.

Leigh's Triangular Landscape

A peaceful walk through the pastoral scenery of Leigh and the upper Mole valley.

Walk 16

•DISTANCE•	4 miles (6.4km)
•MINIMUM TIME•	1hr 45min
•ASCENT / GRADIENT•	73ft (22m) ▲ ▲ ▲
•LEVEL OF DIFFICULTY•	🚶 🚶 🚶
•PATHS•	Field edge and cross field paths, 22 stiles
•LANDSCAPE•	Low lying, small scale agricultural scenery
•SUGGESTED MAP•	aqua3 OS Explorer 146 Dorking, Box Hill & Reigate
•START / FINISH•	Grid reference: TQ 223468
•DOG FRIENDLINESS•	Keep on lead near livestock
•PARKING•	Lay-by between the Plough and church in Leigh
•PUBLIC TOILETS•	None on route

BACKGROUND TO THE WALK

Leigh is one of those places that seems happy for history to pass it by. Indeed, part of its charm is that so little seems to have happened here recently. Your walk starts on the picturesque village green, where the pub, church and adjoining Priest's House all have their origins in the 15th century. Just up the road, Leigh Place may be older still; but in 1530 it was sold to Edward Shelley, an ancestor of the poet. The sale deed records the village as 'Lye' – and that's how the name is pronounced.

What's the Point?

In Tudor times, Leigh was in the heart of Surrey's Black Country. There was a small iron smelting furnace or 'bloomery' here, and the water-powered hammers near Hammer Bridge, to the south of Clayhill Farm, would beat the metal into shape. Later, the dramatist Ben Jonson is said to have lived at Swain's Farm; but by then the place was so quiet that an early 20th century writer wondered what on earth he could have found to do there.

To put Leigh on the map, you must climb to the top of the low hill above Swain's Farm. Here, about a mile into your walk, you'll come to a curious concrete pillar standing aloof near the middle of the field. The column is just one of around 6,500 'triangulation pillars' that, until very recently, formed the basic framework for all Ordnance Survey mapping.

Triangulation relies on a network of triangles with precisely measured sides and angles, like the frame of those geodetic domes that were popular in the 1970s. It all started in the reign of George III, when Major General William Roy was commissioned by the Royal Society to measure the first baseline on Hounslow Heath, now the site of Heathrow Airport.

Roy had campaigned for a national mapping authority, but he died in 1790, a year before the Ordnance Survey was founded. The new organisation built on Roy's work to complete the triangulation of Great Britain, and published its first one-inch-to-the-mile maps during the early years of the 19th century. These were to become the Ordnance Survey's flagship products, progressing through seven different series until being replaced by the modern Landranger maps in the mid-1970s. On the top of the triangulation pillar, you'll see the metal fitment where generations of Ordnance Survey surveyors have fixed their theodolites to check the location of similar pillars on the surrounding hills. But time marches on. At the dawn of the new millennium, the advent of satellite-based global positioning systems (GPS) has transformed map-making technology and consigned most of these hilltop pillars to the history books; some have even been demolished. Leigh can once more return to its slumbers.

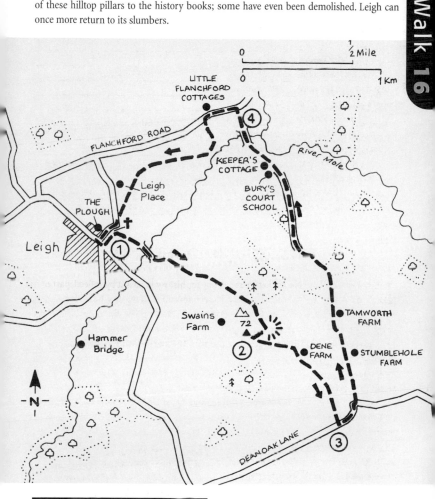

Walk 16 Directions

① With your back to the **Plough**, turn left onto the village green and take the signposted footpath through the churchyard and across an open field to a wooden footbridge. Cross the brook, and the waymarked stile 40yds (37m) further on, then follow the hedge

on your right to the far corner of the field. Jump the stile, and turn left onto a waymarked bridleway.

After 100yds (91m), bear right through a waymarked wicket gate towards another stile. Nip across, and continue straight ahead towards the far corner of the field. Turn right over a waymarked stile, and up the short hill beside the woods. At the brow, you'll come to a stile; don't jump it, but turn right, towards the **triangulation pillar** (or trig point) across the field. As you'd expect, there are some splendid views from here.

② Turn hard left at the triangulation pillar, and double back to the far corner of the field. Yes, you could have kept straight on beside the hedge you were following earlier, but that would have been trespassing! Cross the stile in the corner of the field, then follow the succession of waymarked stiles that lead you to **Dene Farm**, and guide you across the farm drive. Bear half right here, and cross the field to a plank bridge and stile. Continue through the next field, and out onto **Deanoak Lane**.

WHERE TO EAT AND DRINK   ⓘ

The **Plough** in Leigh is your stereotype English country pub, with its pretty flower tubs and pleasant garden. White weatherboarded and tile-hung, it sits comfortably overlooking the village green. There are Hall & Woodhouse ales behind the bar and a huge range of eating options, from bar snacks to restaurant meals. It's open all day at weekends. Dogs are welcome in the public bar and garden and children under 14 in the restaurant and garden.

---

③ Turn left; then, just beyond the double bend, turn left again, up the lane towards **Stumblehole Farm**. Follow the lane straight past **Tamworth Farm** and through a small patch of woodland, then bear left at the three way signpost onto a concrete road.

Continue past **Bury's Court School**; then, 55yds (50m) beyond **Keeper's Cottage**, look out for a metal gate on your right. Climb over here, and

---

WHAT TO LOOK FOR   ⓘ

Take a good look at the west end of **St Bartholomew's Church** as you set off through the churchyard – it has a remarkable history. Much of the church dates from around 1430, when the building was given a low stone tower and weatherboarded belfry. It stood for more than four centuries, until it was replaced by a larger tower when the church was restored in 1855. But the new tower didn't last. In 1890 it was swept away in a dramatic remodelling which extended the nave, and added the western porch and shingled spire which you see today.

---

bear away beside the infant **River Mole**. Follow the waymarked route over a wooden footbridge, and out onto **Flanchford Road**.

④ Turn left, as far as **Little Flanchford Cottages**. A few paces further on, take the footpath on your left, and cross the stile after 150yds (137m). Now bear right across two footbridges, and continue along the right hand edge of the next three fields. Walk diagonally to your left across the fourth field, to a small wicket gate. Turn left here, for the last 100yds (91m) along the road and back to the start.

WHILE YOU'RE THERE   ⓘ

A short drive will bring you to **Reigate Priory Museum**, which shares its impressive location with Reigate Priory School. The priory buildings date from Tudor times, and are set in 65 acres (26.3ha) of parkland on the outskirts of town. Here you'll find changing displays of local history, domestic items and costumes, often displayed in life-like settings that evoke the spirit of their time. The museum's facilities include a gift shop and toilets, and it's open on Wednesday and Saturday afternoons.

Horsing and Coursing on Epsom Downs

A walk across Epsom Downs racecourse that everyone will enjoy.

·DISTANCE·	5 miles (8km)
·MINIMUM TIME·	2hrs
·ASCENT / GRADIENT·	394ft (120m)
·LEVEL OF DIFFICULTY·	
·PATHS·	Mainly broad, easy-to-follow bridleways
·LANDSCAPE·	Open skies of Downs and wooded landscape
·SUGGESTED MAP·	aqua3 OS Explorer 146 Dorking, Box Hill & Reigate
·START / FINISH·	Grid reference: TQ 223584
·DOG FRIENDLINESS·	On lead before midday, when racehorses train on Downs
·PARKING·	Car park by mini-roundabout on Tattenham Corner Rd (charges apply on race days)
·PUBLIC TOILETS·	200yds (183m) west of car park, towards grandstand

BACKGROUND TO THE WALK

There's always a holiday atmosphere on Epsom Downs. With the ice cream vans, the wind in your face, and the huge, wide skies, the Downs have everything but sea and sand. Families come to picnic on the grassy areas inside the course, whilst Biggles wannabees loop the loop with their model aircraft, indifferent to the children's kites in their airspace.

There's a long tradition of recreation on Epsom Downs. In 1660, Samuel Pepys' diary records daily horse races at midday, with wrestling, cudgel-playing, hawking and foot racing in the afternoons. Hare coursing was also popular at about this time, based on an enclosed warren established by Lord Baltimore in 1720. You'll see two of the old gateposts to the Warren on your right, as you walk down beside the gallops a mile or so into your walk.

They're Off!

You'll start by crossing the racecourse itself. The first formal race meeting took place in 1661 in the presence of His Majesty King Charles II, but it was a young man of 21 who was destined to establish the most famous names in Epsom's sporting calendar. In 1773 the 12th Earl of Derby bought the Oaks, a country house at nearby Woodmansterne. He and his friends were keen followers of racing and, in 1779, they inaugurated 'The Oaks' – a new race for three year-old fillies. Spurred on by the success of the new race, the Earl and his friend Sir Charles Bunbury promoted another short distance event the following year. The Earl won the toss for the honour of naming the contest, though Sir Charles consoled himself when his horse Diomed actually won the race. The Epsom Derby had been born.

The Bluck of the Devil

But what of the spectators? To begin with there were minimal facilities, and the 18th-century crowds simply gathered on the hill. Enter the property speculator Charles Bluck; a 'rogue and a rascal, an unscrupulous knave, the biggest villain to go unhanged'. Bluck charmed the Lord of the Manor with his plans for a new £5,000 grandstand, and quickly obtained the lease to a prime 1 acre (0.4ha) site. This upstaged the newly formed Epsom Grandstand Association, and there was a good deal of wheeling and dealing before the Association completed its stand in 1830. The building lasted for almost a century, until the site was redeveloped in 1927. The new Queen's Stand, added in 1992, includes facilities for conferences, dances and corporate hospitality. Twice a month throughout the summer, you can even go behind the scenes with the Derby Experience Tour for a glimpse of life and history at the world's most famous racecourse. Recreation on the Downs has come of age.

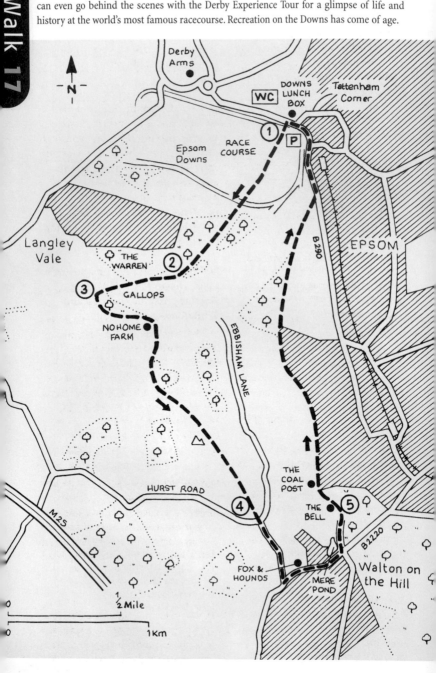

Walk 17 Directions

① From the mini-roundabout near the **Downs Lunch Box**, take the signposted bridleway to **Walton Road**. Cross the race course and continue along the broad, waymarked lane, keeping an eye out for the occasional car. The bridleway remains open on race days, though naturally there are some restrictions during the races.

WHAT TO LOOK FOR   ⓘ

Just north of the Bell at Withybed Corner, you'll pass a white-painted cast iron post with the City of London coat of arms near the top. There are over 200 of these '**coal posts**' around London, with a history going back to the Great Fire of 1666. The cost of rebuilding after the fire was so enormous that a levy was imposed on coal brought into the City. It took until 1834 to repay the debt, after which the revenue helped to fund drainage improvements in the capital. Originally the tax was collected in the Port of London but, with the growth of road and rail transport, cast iron posts were erected in 1861 to mark the taxation boundary. The levy was discontinued in 1890.

---

② At length the lane swings hard right, and you follow the waymarked bridleway as it forks off down a narrow path to the left. Bear right at the gallops, continuing beside a rustic wooden fence before rejoining the broader lane down past the **Warren**. There's a lovely view across the valley from here, and you can spot the spire of **Headley church** on the horizon.

③ At the bottom of the hill, near the 'Racehorses Only' sign, lies a six-way junction. Think of it as a mini-roundabout, and take the third exit, straight ahead. It's a narrow track through scrubby trees, but it soon leads you out between wooden posts onto a broader bridleway. Turn left and then, in a few paces, fork left. Keep straight on at the bridleway signpost, towards **Walton on the Hill**, and follow the waymarked track as it swings right at **Nohome Farm** and begins the long climb out of the valley.

④ The bridleway ends at the **Cotton Mills**, at the junction of Hurst Road and Ebbisham Lane. Keep on down **Ebbisham Lane**, and turn left at the bottom into **Walton Street**. Pass the **Fox and Hounds** and **Mere Pond**, then turn left at The Bell pub sign, up the side of the pond. After 30yds (27m), fork right at **Withybed Corner** and follow the lane to **The Bell**.

⑤ Keep straight on, along the path signposted to **Motts Hill Lane**. Continue past the coal post and **White Cottage**; then, as the lane bears right, turn left onto the bridleway. From here you simply follow the waymarked route all the way back to **Epsom Lane North**. Journey's end is now in sight; cross the road, and continue along the pavement towards the car park. It finishes 100yds (91m) before you reach the car park, so do take care.

WHERE TO EAT AND DRINK   ⓘ

Just across the road from the car park, you'll see the **Lunch Box** kiosk and the large **Tattenham Corner** pub/restaurant overlooking the course. Tucked away behind the grandstand, the **Derby Arms** is quieter and more intimate, though still with the emphasis on food. At the other end of your walk, the lively **Fox and Hounds** in Walton on the Hill is your best bet for a bite to eat. You'll also pass **The Bell**, a small, drinkers pub tucked away from the road at Withybed Corner.

Walk 18

Have You Seen What's On the Box?

As well as its famous box trees, Box Hill has its own place in television history.

•DISTANCE•	4 miles (6.4km)
•MINIMUM TIME•	2hrs 15min
•ASCENT / GRADIENT•	803ft (245m) ▲▲▲
•LEVEL OF DIFFICULTY•	𝕩𝕩 𝕩𝕩 𝕩
•PATHS•	Woodland tracks, with two sections on minor roads
•LANDSCAPE•	Mainly wooded, but with some breathtaking views
•SUGGESTED MAP•	aqua3 OS Explorer 146 Dorking, Box Hill & Reigate
•START / FINISH•	Grid reference: TQ 178513
•DOG FRIENDLINESS•	Some roadside sections and grazing animals
•PARKING•	National Trust car park, Fort Cottages, Box Hill Country Park
•PUBLIC TOILETS•	At the start

BACKGROUND TO THE WALK

Just after leaving the car park, you'll notice a drive to a private house on your right. This is Swiss Cottage, home to John Logie Baird during the 1920s and 1930s. Baird had trained as an electrical engineer, but spent his early life on a variety of hare-brained projects that ranged from curing piles to producing jams and mango chutney. He was the archetypal absent-minded professor; scruffy, permanently short of cash, and given to sketching on restaurant table cloths or changing his socks in public.

It's Television, Jim, But Not As We Know It
Baird's prototype for a mechanical television was pure Wallace and Gromit. On top of an old tea chest, he set up a scanning disc cut from a hatbox, spinning on an old darning needle driven by an electric motor. There was a lamp in an empty biscuit tin and some fourpenny bull's eye lenses, all held together with sealing wax and string. But it worked, and in 1925 he unveiled his 'Televisor' at Selfridges in London.

No story about an inventor would be complete without an explosion, and Baird obliged by blowing up his lodgings in Hastings. He moved to London, and then to Box Hill, where he continued to demonstrate inventions like the 'Noctovisor', a night vision infra-red viewer that looked just like a Dalek with no clothes on.

Auntie Takes a Hand
Towards the end of 1929, Baird overcame the BBC's scepticism and began experimental transmissions under their famous 2LO call sign. It was always an uneasy relationship, with Baird continuing to promote mechanically-scanned television at a time when pure electronic systems were being developed on the far side of the Atlantic. EMI launched its 'Emitron' camera in 1935 and, in the following year, the BBC began a new round of test transmissions from Alexandra Palace in south London. Baird and Marconi-EMI were now head to head, broadcasting from adjacent studios on alternate days. The service was

officially opened using Baird's system in November 1936, transmitting two hours of programmes each day. But the two techniques were still running turn and turn about, and it soon became clear that Marconi-EMI had the upper hand. Within three months, the Government had decided that Britain should adopt their electronic system as the new standard for television transmission.

Baird was down, but not out. In the years before his death in 1946, he continued to experiment with big screen television for cinemas, as well as colour and stereoscopic television. Although he never achieved commercial success, Baird is generally remembered as one of the most influential pioneers in British television.

Walk 18 Directions

① Turn left out of the car park, cross over, and follow the roadside path for ½ mile (800m). Shortly after you set out, you'll see a path leading down to the viewpoint, built in memory of Leopold

Salomons of Norbury Park. The commanding views of Dorking and the Mole Valley are well worth the short diversion.

② A few paces short of the **Boxhills Tavern**, re-cross the road and turn off to the left onto the signposted public bridleway. Ignore all the

Walk 18

turnings you pass, and follow the signposted route as it drops down through **Juniper Bottom** to the **Headley Road**.

③ The next few hundred paces are very steep indeed. As an alternative, you can turn left onto **Headley Road**, and rejoin the route by turning left onto the **Old London Road**. This will cut out **Mickleham** village, and shorten your walk by ¾ mile (1.2km).

> ### WHILE YOU'RE THERE ⓘ
> England's largest wine estate lies just a stone's throw from Box Hill. With its 265 acres (107ha) of Mole Valley vineyards and a massive winery and visitor centre, **Denbies** is a place you really shouldn't miss. Drop in for tea or a light lunch in the atrium garden conservatory, or do the full tour, complete with audio-visuals and people mover train. Naturally, the tour ends with a wine tasting in the Denbies cellars, but you can also try before you buy in the winery shop. And if you fancy another walk, there's even a fascinating vineyard trail.

Otherwise, cross straight over onto the public footpath and steel yourself for the seemingly interminable climb up a long flight of rustic steps. Just beyond the top of the steps the path bears right and the gradient eases slightly. Soon you will come to a bench seat. There are splendid views down the Mole Valley and across to Denbies vineyard from here, and I never saw a better excuse for a rest.

Now follow the National Trust's '**long walk**' waymarks as you bear left and drop down over a footpath crossroads with the **Thames Down Link**. Clamber over the stile at the foot of the hill, and continue past the church into the village of **Mickleham**. Turn left, and follow the **Old London Road**. There's a pavement on the right-hand side to begin with, which at times transforms itself into a pleasant rural path running just a few paces away from the road. By the time you reach the junction with the **Zig Zag Road**, it's just an ordinary pavement again.

④ Cross over to the junction with the **Zig Zag Road**, and join the signposted bridleway that climbs steadily all the way back up the hill to the National Trust centre. Near the top, you'll see the old Victorian fort on your right. Turn right at the top of the hill for the last 60yds (55m) back to the car park.

> ### WHERE TO EAT AND DRINK ⓘ
> You'll find a good range of hot and cold drinks, snacks and ices at the open air **National Trust servery** at the start of this walk. There are benches and picnic tables here, too. Down in Mickleham village, you're as likely to hear orders for a glass of Chardonnay as for a pint of real ale. But walkers get a warm welcome at the 16th-century **Running Horses**; the sandwiches are excellent, and there's also a reasonably priced bar menu.

> ### WHAT TO LOOK FOR ⓘ
> Near the top of the hill at the end of the walk, keep an eye out on your right for **Box Hill Fort**. Ancient though it seems, the fort is little more than a century old. It was built in 1899 as one of a line of 13 similar centres strung out along the North Downs, to guard London from the threat of an invasion from mainland Europe. The fort was never permanently manned, but was used as an arms store and muster centre. It is now being conserved by the National Trust but, because bats have colonised the underground ammunition chambers, it isn't open to the public.

Denbies and the Mole Gap

A longer walk in the Mole Gap that includes the famous stepping stones.
See map and information panel for Walk 18

•DISTANCE•	6¼ miles (10km)
•MINIMUM TIME•	2hrs 30min
•ASCENT / GRADIENT•	984ft (300m) ▲▲▲
•LEVEL OF DIFFICULTY•	👫 👫 👫

Walk 19 Directions
(Walk 18 option)

Leave the main route at Point ④, cross the road, and follow the Thames Down Link beside the **Old London Road**. Continue past the **Burford Bridge Hotel**, along the A24, and through the subway. Turn right into **Westhumble Street**, and carry on over the railway bridge into **Chapel Lane**. Beyond the houses, look out for the ruins of **Westhumble Chapel** on your left.

WHAT TO LOOK FOR ⓘ

The overgrown ruins of **Westhumble Chapel** look like one of those romantic, early Victorian watercolours. The little flint built chapel was founded in the late 12th century for worshippers who couldn't cross the river to Mickleham church. It's been ruined for over 500 years, and only the gable walls at the east and west ends now survive to any height. The building was given to the National Trust in 1937.

Immediately beyond the chapel, Point ④, turn left up the bridleway towards **Ashleigh Grange**. Climb steadily to a line of electricity pylons, and follow the drive as it swings to the left. After 80yds (73m), fork left onto the waymarked path and continue for a further 100yds (91m), Point ⑧.

Turn left onto the **North Downs Way National Trail**. After 400yds (366m), look out for a footpath to Dorking. You can visit **Denbies winery** by turning right here and following the path to the main winery building. Otherwise, keep straight on under the railway to the A24. Here, you should turn left, cross via the subway that you used earlier, then walk back to the other side of the main road. Continue through the car park, and cross the **River Mole** via the stepping stones. Alternatively, there's a footbridge 100yds (91m) upstream.

From here, there's only one way to go – the **North Downs Way** hurls itself at **Box Hill**, up flight after flight of unremitting rustic steps. Swing right at the top of the steps, and climb gently for another 200yds (183m) to the viewpoint. Turn hard left here, and double back for the last 150yds (137m) to the car park.

WHERE TO EAT AND DRINK ⓘ

If you like fast food, then **Ryka's** restaurant, just off the Burford Bridge roundabout, is for you. It's serves all-day breakfasts, hot and cold drinks. A little further on, the **Stepping Stones** in Westhumble Street seems reminiscent of a town pub, but there's a good bar menu including Indonesian satay, alongside the traditional favourites.

A Trail Around Dorking Town

A look around ancient and modern Dorking and its countryside setting.

•DISTANCE•	3 miles (4.8km)
•MINIMUM TIME•	1hr 30mins
•ASCENT / GRADIENT•	262ft (80m) ▲▲ ▲ ▲
•LEVEL OF DIFFICULTY•	👣 👣 👣
•PATHS•	Mainly paved streets, with easy section of woodland paths
•LANDSCAPE•	Woodland scenery, parkland and busy town centre
•SUGGESTED MAP•	Dorking town plan, free from Dorking Halls
•START / FINISH•	Grid reference: TQ 171497
•DOG FRIENDLINESS•	Not what most dogs think of as a great day out
•PARKING•	Reigate Road pay-and-display car park, Dorking
•PUBLIC TOILETS•	Dorking Halls

Walk 20 Directions

From the car park, turn left along **Reigate Road**, pass the **Dorking Halls**, and turn left into **Moores Road**. Follow the right hand pavement all the way round until you reach the almshouses, a Victorian replacement for the original 17th-century buildings.

This is Cotmandene, a wide, open area that brings the countryside

WHILE YOU'RE THERE ⓘ

It isn't every town that can boast a network of **underground caves**, so here's something that you really shouldn't miss. On one Sunday each month, you can descend up to 76ft (23m) into the gloom, on a candle-lit guided tour through the maze of artificial passages weaving its way under the town centre. Nowadays some of the caves are used as storage cellars but, in earlier times, these were the haunts of smugglers and outlawed religious sects. More information can be got from the Dorking Halls Box Office.

right into town. Cottagers once grazed their animals here, and local people still exercise their right to dry washing on a cluster of metal poles on the green.

From the almshouses, walk across the grass to **Chart Lane** and turn left. Follow the pavement as far as the A24, then cross **Chart Lane** and bear right into the **Glory Wood**. As the footpath climbs away from the road, steer as right as you can, ignoring turnings off to the left. Leave the woods at the wooden gates, and fork right. There's a bench here, and a fine view towards Ranmore church spire in the woods on the horizon.

Drop down past St Paul's School, cross **St Paul's Road**, and dive down the little footpath directly opposite. Keep straight on into **Chequers Place**; then, after 70yds (64m), turn off down a narrow alley on your left. This brings you to **Rose Hill**, almost as pretty as its name; walk around the green, and out into

Walk 20

South Street through the mock-Tudor **Rose Hill Arch** at the foot of the hill.

On your right is the **Bulls Head**. Charles Dickens is generally reckoned to have used the local coachman William Broad as the model for his character in *The Pickwick Papers*. In the 19th century, Broad ran a daily service from here to London at a fare of five shillings (25p in today's money) for outside passengers, or seven shillings (35p) for softies travelling inside the coach.

Turn left and walk round to the war memorial opposite Waitrose. Just to the left of the memorial, you'll see the little blue door at the entrance to **Dorking Caves**. Cross the zebra crossing and turn left, then right into **Junction Road**. Cross over at the bottom and turn right into **West Street**.

While you're here, look out for the plaque on William Mullins' house. A shoemaker by trade, Mullins sold up in 1619, and set sail with his family on the Mayflower in the following year. Tragically, Mullins, his wife and son all fell ill soon after reaching the New World, and died just two months later. Just off **West Street** on your left, **Dorking Museum** occupies the old foundry site dating from John Bartlett's blacksmithy and forge of the 1820s.

Continue into **High Street**, and wander down the little alley next to Barclays Bank to **St Martins Church**, designed by Henry Woodyer and completed in 1877. The flintwork alone is worth a look and, inside, the church positively oozes with high Victorian art. Further up the **High Street**, the new **St Martins Walk** shopping precinct is a refreshing antidote to the usual run of monolithic shopping malls that disfigure so many country towns.

A few paces further on, turn left down **Mill Lane**. Fork right at the bottom towards the **Meadowbank recreation ground**, then turn right again beside the brook. Keep the lake on your left and veer right, over a girder bridge and out onto **London Road**. Turn left; then, after 100yds (91m), turn right at the **Court House**, and follow the drive as it winds up past the library and Council Offices, back to the **Reigate Road**. Cross over, back to the car park at the start.

Walk 21

The Headley Heath Highlanders

A circular tour through an 8,000 year-old landscape.

•DISTANCE•	4½ miles (7.2km)
•MINIMUM TIME•	2hrs 15min
•ASCENT / GRADIENT•	425ft (160m) ▲▲▲
•LEVEL OF DIFFICULTY•	🚶🚶 🚶🚶 🚶🚶
•PATHS•	Mainly woodland tracks
•LANDSCAPE•	Wooded heathland and chalk valleys
•SUGGESTED MAP•	aqua3 OS Explorer 146 Dorking, Box Hill & Reigate
•START / FINISH•	Grid reference: TQ 205538
•DOG FRIENDLINESS•	Take care near grazing animals on heath
•PARKING•	National Trust car park, Headley Heath
•PUBLIC TOILETS•	None on route

BACKGROUND TO THE WALK

Look around you, for this is no ordinary place. About a tenth of all the world's lowland heaths are found in southern England, and Headley includes the largest remaining area of acid heathland on the North Downs. Although heathland is an artificial habitat, it's home to many rare and threatened species. Go quietly, and you may see stonechats, woodlarks and even the occasional Dartford warbler. Common lizards live here too, as well as slow worms. These plain, silvery little legless lizards are often mistaken for snakes, though in fact they're completely harmless.

Unnatural History

The name Headley means a heather clearing surrounded by woodland, and that's pretty much what you'll see here today. But, around 8,000 years ago, this was a very different landscape. At that time most of Britain was covered with dense woodland and, without human intervention, that's how it would have stayed. Things altered when Neolithic people arrived in about 6000 BC, slashing and burning the forest to provide grazing for their animals. At Headley, they found just what they wanted; high ground, with an easily worked sandy soil. It was the beginning of organised farming and, in one way or another, the land has been grazed here ever since.

Well, almost. Photographs taken during the first half of the 20th century still show an open landscape of heather, gorse and bracken, with scarcely a tree in sight. But all that changed during the Second World War, when Headley Heath was used as a training area by the Canadian Army. Their tanks and earth moving equipment destroyed the open vegetation and, after the war, birch trees started to invade the disturbed ground. Now, Headley Heath is the setting for a very different type of warfare – the constant battle against encroaching woodland.

You'll see the National Trust's secret weapon as you walk around the heath. The brown woolly Highland cattle are probably related to the Celtic Longhorns once used by Scottish crofters to provide meat, milk, clothing and motive power. The Trust currently has 14 of these natural lawnmowers, keeping down the scrub in their two constantly moving enclosures. When I was last there, they were west of the car park, and near the little pond close to the start of the walk; however, the long term aim is to graze up to 35 cattle in a single large paddock. Besides chomping through the lower vegetation, these animals will happily push over 20ft (6m) birch trees and munch off the leaves. Their long, curved horns are every bit as fearsome as they look, so please treat the animals with respect.

Walk 21 Directions

① Face the road, walk to the far right-hand corner of the car park, and take the bridleway on your right. Pass a bench and follow the track past a pond to a crossroads.

② Turn right here, and follow the waymarked route down to a parting of the ways at the foot of the hill.

Fork right along the National Trust's waymarked route, and follow it over a low rise and down to a crossroads in the valley bottom.

Turn left along a waymarked bridleway that climbs gently round to the left. After 100yds (91m) turn right, following the waymarked route that leaves the track and climbs steeply up through the woods to a National Trust sign,

Walk 21

half hidden in the trees. If you reach the road at **High Ashurst**, you've gone too far; turn back, and fork left after 50yds (46m).

③ Double back to the right, and wind your way down out of the woods. Cross **Lodgebottom Road** at **Cockshot Cottage**, and climb steeply up the narrow path to a T-junction with a good, level track.

WHERE TO EAT AND DRINK ⓘ

You'll find a good range of hot and cold snacks, teas and ices at the **refreshment caravan** in the car park at the start. It's open Tuesday to Sunday, all year round. Then, three-quarters of the way round the walk, you'll come to the **Cock Horse**, next to Headley church. This has a traditional public bar as well as a more food-orientated area. The nearby **village stores** also serves teas, coffees, cakes and snacks.

WHAT TO LOOK FOR ⓘ

Headley churchyard boasts an odd little grotto, quite different from anything you're likely to see anywhere else. It's actually the Faithfull family vault. Ferdinand Faithfull was Rector of Headley during the mid-19th century; Emily Faithfull, who was born at Headley's Old Rectory in 1835, established a women's printing press and later became Printer-in-Ordinary to Queen Victoria. Like the tower of the present Victorian church, the vault was built using flints from the original church, which was demolished in 1858. Inside is a small font, and slate tablets inscribed with the Ten Commandments.

---

④ Turn right, and follow the track as far as **Mill Way**. Just short of the road, bear right onto the horse margin and follow it until it leads you across the road and onto a signposted byway.

⑤ If you don't want to visit **Headley** village, turn right at the end of the byway, and rejoin the route at Point ⑥. Otherwise fork left here, into **Slough Lane**, and walk up to the junction with **Church Lane**. Turn right onto the permissive bridleway that runs beside the road.

Just past the **Cock Horse**, fork right at the bus stop onto a signposted footpath. Follow it through to a road junction, turn hard right into **Leech Lane**, and drop down to the junction with **Tumber Street**.

⑥ Turn left and cross **Mill Way** into **Crabtree Lane**. Follow the waymarked horse track past **Broom House**, and up the hill to a pit on your left hand side. Bear left here, along the blue waymarked track. Pass a group of houses on your left and continue for 275yds (251m), until you see the car park between the trees on your left hand side. Turn left for the short stroll back to your car.

WHILE YOU'RE THERE ⓘ

For something a bit different, take a look around **Reigate Castle** grounds, just a few miles from Headley. The castle was built soon after the Norman Conquest, and strengthened in the 13th century. During the Civil Wars it was garrisoned first by the Royalists, and then by Cromwell's supporters. After that the building gradually fell derelict, but the grounds were renovated and a mock gateway was added during the 18th century. Beneath the castle lies the mysterious Baron's Cave, 'an extraordinary passage with a vaulted roof hewn with great labour out of the soft stone'. No one seems to know exactly why the cave was built, but there's a local tradition that the Barons met here whilst drawing up the Magna Carta in 1215.

Royal Romances at Polesden Lacey

A woodland circuit around a great country house that was once a favourite with high society.

•DISTANCE•	4¼ miles (7km)
•MINIMUM TIME•	2hrs 15min
•ASCENT / GRADIENT•	607ft (185m)
•LEVEL OF DIFFICULTY•	
•PATHS•	Woodland and farm tracks
•LANDSCAPE•	Remote wooded valleys around Polesden Lacey estate
•SUGGESTED MAP•	aqua3 OS Explorer 146 Dorking, Box Hill & Reigate
•START / FINISH•	Grid reference: TQ 141503
•DOG FRIENDLINESS•	The kind of walk that dogs dream about
•PARKING•	National Trust car park on Ranmore Common Road
•PUBLIC TOILETS•	Toilets at Polesden Lacey for visitors only

BACKGROUND TO THE WALK

To say that the history of Polesden Lacey is the history of the British monarchy through the early decades of the 20th century is, perhaps, overstating things. Nevertheless, in the years before the Second World War the royal family's footfalls often echoed within these sumptuous walls.

Your Personal Tour

Even if you don't step beyond the Lacey's main gates, there's plenty of opportunity to see the house and grounds as you weave your way around the estate. Soon after the start of the walk, you'll get a stunning panorama across the terrace and formal lawns to the colonnaded south front, and you'll be glad of a pair of binoculars here. A little further on, you'll dive under the thatched bridge linking the formal gardens to the summer house and the old kitchen garden, and pass the entrance to the Home Farm. Then comes the main entrance at North Lodge, before you turn south and drop under the balustraded bridge that carries the drive from Chapel Lane.

Polesden Reborn

Late in the 18th century, the dramatist Richard Sheridan made his home at Polesden Lacey. Although he thought that it was 'the nicest place, within prudent distance of town, in England', the house was pulled down after his death. In 1823 a new Regency villa arose on the site, and this building now forms the core of the modern house. The Hon Ronald and Mrs Greville bought Polesden Lacey in 1906, extended and remodelled the house and its grounds, and set about transforming their new home into a focus of high society.

Royal Romances

The couple were not exactly without influence. King Edward VII was an intimate friend, and the cream of Edwardian aristocracy was drawn to Polesden Lacey by the stimulating company and Mrs Greville's impeccable hospitality. The royal family were frequent visitors throughout the inter-war years and the Duke and Duchess of York – later King George VI and Queen Elizabeth (the Queen Mother) – came here for part of their honeymoon in 1923.

Ten years later, another royal romance ended in tears. The Prince of Wales was a particular favourite of Mrs Greville's but, by the mid-1930s, his liaison with the American divorcee Mrs Wallis Simpson was causing speculation on both sides of the Atlantic. When King George V died in 1936, and the new King declared his intention of marriage, it unleashed a constitutional storm that led to his abdication before the year's end.

Time was also running out for Polesden Lacey. Mrs Greville had just a few years left to live, and she bequeathed her home to the National Trust in 1942.

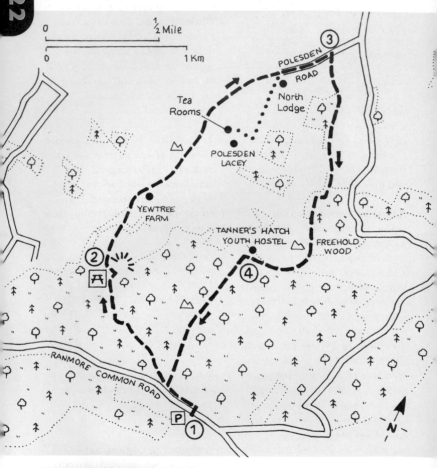

Walk 22 Directions

① Cross the road from the car park, turn left, and walk for 200yds (183m) along the broad roadside verge. Turn right just beyond the tile-hung **Fox Cottages**, where two

public footpaths meet the road. Take the left-hand path through the woods and, ignoring all turnings, follow it through a little combe. At length it draws alongside a post and rail fence, and veers sharp left. Turn right here, through the gap in the fence, and continue through the

Walk 22

woodland glade. Just beyond a wooden gate, turn left onto the signposted **Yewtree Farm Walk**. Continue to the gravelled forest track 100yds (91m) further on, and turn right.

A little further on you'll come to a bench seat on your right. There's a great view of **Polesden Lacey** from here, and it's a good spot for a picnic. Notice the massive estate water tower sticking up through the trees, just to the left of the main house.

② Follow the gravelled track as it winds past **Yewtree Farm**; then, 150yds (137m) beyond the farm, fork left. Follow the signposted bridleway across a low causeway until it climbs to meet an estate road. Keep straight on, under a little thatched timber footbridge.

As you pass the entrance to **Home Farm House**, look half left across the open field. On the far horizon, you'll see a long, low white building – and, on a clear day, you'll be able to pick out the jets landing in front of it at Heathrow. Bear gently right

past the entrance drive to **Polesden Lacey**, and continue onto **Polesden Road**. Walk right to the end of the broad, grass verge on the right hand side of the road; then, 60yds (55m) further on, turn right down a waymarked bridleway towards the youth hostel.

③ The track is relatively easy to follow. It zig-zags right and left into **Freehold Wood**, then dives under a stone-arched bridge. Continue down the sunken way, then bear right at the blue waymarker post at the bottom of the hill and climb up gently through the woods to **Tanner's Hatch**.

④ Bear left at the youth hostel and follow the yellow waymarked gravel track as it climbs up gently but steadily all the way back to **Ranmore Common Road**. Turn left for the last 200yds (183m) back to the car park.

WHILE YOU'RE THERE ⓘ

You can easily include a visit to **Polesden Lacey** in this walk, which passes the main entrance. The principal rooms in this magnificent mansion are the natural setting for Mrs Greville's collections of paintings, furniture, silver and porcelain, now displayed just as you'd have seen them at one of her Edwardian house parties. Outside, the formal gardens and lawns are the perfect counterpoint to your woodland walk.

WHERE TO EAT AND DRINK ⓘ

The licensed **National Trust tea room** in Polesden Lacey's old stable block serves teas, coffees, and light lunches, as well as a nice selection of home made cakes and scones. Tuck yourself into a table in one of the cleverly converted horses' stalls, or sit out in the spacious, sunny courtyard.

Friday Street; Fact, or Fiction?

Through woodland to the highest point in south east England.

•DISTANCE•	5¼ miles (8.4km)
•MINIMUM TIME•	2hrs 30min
•ASCENT / GRADIENT•	640ft (195m) ▲▲ ▲
•LEVEL OF DIFFICULTY•	🚶🚶 🚶🚶 🚶
•PATHS•	Easily walked woodland tracks, but poor waymarking
•LANDSCAPE•	Ancient landscape of thickly wooded sandstone heaths
•SUGGESTED MAP•	aqua3 OS Explorer 146 Dorking, Box Hill & Reigate
•START / FINISH•	Grid reference: TQ 130432
•DOG FRIENDLINESS•	Can mostly run free
•PARKING•	Woodland parking at Starveall Corner
•PUBLIC TOILETS•	None on route

BACKGROUND TO THE WALK

Somewhere in the forgotten landscape of thickly wooded sandstone heaths around Abinger Common lies Friday Street, Surrey's smallest, prettiest, and most remote hamlet. Friday Street's most famous son is an enigmatic figure who blends life and legend with the effortless ease of King Arthur. There's no denying Stephan Langton's place in the history books. He was born around 1150, and orphaned by the age of ten. His parents may have come from Lincolnshire, though legend has it that he was born in Friday Street.

A Leading Scholar

It's clear that Stephan was educated by monks, but although one source has him singing in the local choir, it seems that he also studied at the University of Paris. Here, it's said, he established himself as a leading theologian; a plausible theory, since Stephan went on to become Archbishop of Canterbury. By the time he was 18, Stephan was living in Albury, just a few miles down the road from Friday Street. Here he fell in love with Alice, and legend has it that the couple were strolling in the nearby woods when they were set upon by King John and his followers. There's a problem with the story here, since John was by now about 12 months old, and didn't come to the throne for another 30 years. But it's a good story…

John kidnapped Alice, and took her off to his hunting lodge at Tangley, near Guildford. Stephan followed the trail and set fire to the house in an attempt to rescue his sweetheart but, in the confusion, the girl fainted or was overcome by smoke. Thinking her dead, Stephan wandered off to become a monk. By the dawn of the 13th century, we're back on firmer ground. Not without reason, the idle and self-centred King John was deeply unpopular. He refused to accept Stephan Langton as the Pope's choice of Archbishop of Canterbury, provoking six years of conflict with Rome and the threat of a French invasion. By 1214 the King had capitulated, but he now faced a baronial revolt. Langton stepped in as mediator; he was prominent in drafting the Magna Carta, and was amongst the signatories at Runnymede in 1215. Meanwhile, Alice recovered from her ordeal and went on to become Abbess of St Catherine's in Guildford. Some years later, the couple were unexpectedly reunited after Mass at St Martha's Chapel near Guildford. But don't expect a happy ending - the Abbess was so overcome with emotion that she died in Stephan's arms.

Walk **23**

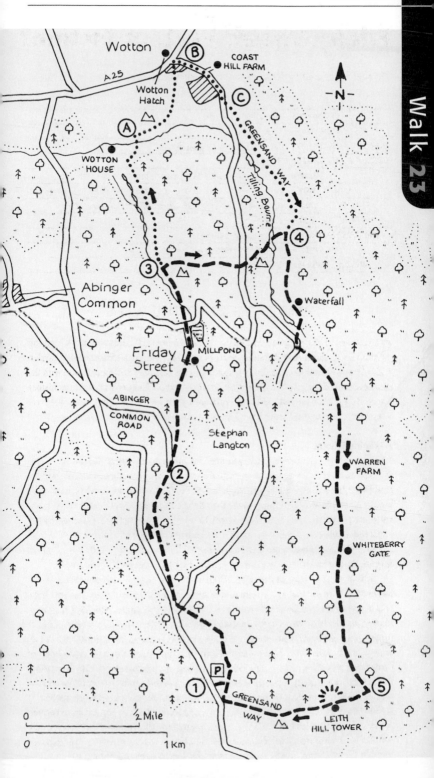

Wotton

Ⓑ COAST HILL FARM

A25

Wotton Hatch

Ⓒ

Ⓐ

GREENSAND WAY

WOTTON HOUSE

Tilling Bourne

-N-

Ⓓ

Abinger Common

Ⓒ

Ⓒ

Waterfall

Friday Street

MILLPOND

ABINGER COMMON ROAD

Stephan Langton

Ⓒ

WARREN FARM

WHITEBERRY GATE

Ⓟ

Ⓒ

GREENSAND WAY

Ⓒ

LEITH HILL TOWER

0   ½ Mile

0   1 Km

Walk 23 Directions

① Leave the car park at the gate near the top left-hand corner. After 45yds (41m), turn left onto a woodland path and follow it to a crossroads. Turn left and drop down to a road junction. Take the road towards **Abinger Common** and **Wotton**; then, 90yds (82m) further on, turn onto the narrow, unsignposted path on your right. Cross a tarmac drive, and continue as it widens into a woodland ride.

WHILE YOU'RE THERE   ⓘ

In return for climbing the 75 spiral steps of **Leith Hill Tower** you'll get a view that stretches from the London Eye to the coast. Built in 1766 by Richard Hull of Leith Hill Place it's popularly believed he wanted to raise the 967ft (295m) hill to exactly 1,000ft (305m). After his death in 1772, he was buried beneath its floor. During the next hundred years the tower was raised to its present height of 1,029ft (329m), and the staircase and battlements were added. The National Trust has owned it since 1923, and has an information room on the first floor.

---

② Leave the woods and continue briefly along **Abinger Common Road**. When you reach a house called **St John's**, fork right onto the bridleway and follow it through to **Friday Street**. Pass the pub and the millpond, and drop down past the letter box at Pond Cottage. Follow the rough track towards **Wotton**, bear left past **Yew Tree Cottage**, and continue until you reach a gate.

WHAT TO LOOK FOR   ⓘ

Shortly after you join the Greensand Way you'll see an impressive waterfall on your left, cascading 65ft (20m) into a pool. It's fed by a leat from Brookmill Pond and was built around 1738 as part of an ambitious landscaping project.

---

③ Turn right over the stile, and climb the sandy track into the woods. Soon it levels off, bears left past a young plantation, then veers right at the far end. Two stiles carry you across **Sheephouse Lane**, and soon you're dropping to another stile. Nip over, and follow the fence across the **Tilling Bourne** until you reach two steps up to a stile.

④ Cross the stile, and turn right onto the **Greensand Way**. It brushes the road at the **Triple Bar Riding Centre** then turns left onto a public bridleway. Keep right at the National Trust's **Henman Base Camp**, and right again at **Warren Farm**, where the forest road ends.

Here the waymarked **Greensand Way** forks right again, along the narrow woodland track. Keep ahead when you come to the bench and three-way signpost at **Whiteberry Gate**, climbing steadily at first, then more steeply, until you come to a barrier and five-way junction.

WHERE TO EAT AND DRINK   ⓘ

The **Stephan Langton** in Friday Street is a great walkers' pub serving filled croissants, pies and children's meals – and fabulous burgers. There's a refreshment kiosk in **Leith Hill Tower** where you'll find hot and cold drinks, as well as cakes and sandwiches.

---

⑤ The way ahead dives steeply down; turn right, still following the waymarked **Greensand Way** as it pushes up towards **Leith Hill Tower**. Pass the tower, taking the left-hand fork towards **Starveall Corner**. Follow the broad track back to the barrier at **Leith Hill Road**, then swing right onto the signposted bridleway. After 140yds (128m), turn left for the last little stretch back to the car park.

And on to Wotton

A longer walk through the attractive setting of John Evelyn's family home.
See map and information panel for Walk 23

•DISTANCE•	6½ miles (10.4km)
•MINIMUM TIME•	3hrs
•ASCENT / GRADIENT•	185ft (607m) ▲▲ ▲ ▲
•LEVEL OF DIFFICULTY•	🚶 🚶 🚶

Walk 24 Directions (Walk 23 option)

Leave Walk 23 at Point ③, and carry straight on over the stile beside the gate. The vistas are more open as you approach **Wotton House** and, for company, an attractive chain of ornamental pools runs though the valley less than 100yds (91m) from the track.

The route narrows as you approach **Wotton House**, then swings to the right and drops down to a footpath crossroads. Keep straight on, down the narrowest of the paths, then nip over the stile and follow the field edge to a second stile, Point ④. Look to the left here for some good views of Wotton House. Cross the stile onto the drive to **Wotton House**, turn right, and climb steadily to a large 'Private' notice. Here you must leave the drive, jump the stile on your right, and bear left across the field. Nip over the stile at the far side, and follow the right of way through the **Wotton Hatch car park** to the A25 junction with Damphurst Lane, Point ⑧.

> **WHERE TO EAT AND DRINK** ℹ️
> With its wooden floors and pleasant garden, the ivy-covered **Wotton Hatch** is a landmark on the A25. It follows the successful Vintage Inns formula, but is none the worse for that; you'll get decent beer, and honest, well presented meals.

Turn right into **Damphurst Lane**. After 285yds (260m), you'll reach the entrance to **Coast Hill Farm**. Turn in to the left, and follow the waymarked footpath that runs alongside the road until it brings you to a lodge cottage, Point ©. Walk up the cottage drive and, after 40yds (37m), fork left onto the waymarked **Greensand Way**. Now, simply follow the track until you rejoin the main route at Point ④.

> **WHAT TO LOOK FOR** ℹ️
> The diarist John Evelyn was born in **Wotton House** in 1620, and you'll get some good views of the house and grounds on this walk. But there was more to the man than his diary, which wasn't published until more than a century after his death. He trained as a lawyer and was a friend of Samuel Pepys. In his own lifetime, Evelyn was best known for his book *Sylva, or a Discourse of Forest Trees*. His interests included architecture and gardening; he was involved in landscaping the family estates at Wotton, and also helped to plan the gardens at nearby Albury Park. Towards the end of his life he returned to Wotton and lived with his brother. He inherited the estate in 1699, and died in 1706.

Trails from the Riverbank

Off the water or on it, you'll find plenty of interest on this fascinating section of the Thames Path between Walton-on-Thames and Hampton Court.

•DISTANCE•	5 miles (8km)
•MINIMUM TIME•	2hrs
•ASCENT / GRADIENT•	Negligible
•LEVEL OF DIFFICULTY•	
•PATHS•	Level, well maintained tow path walk, ideal for young families with a pushchair, and active wheelchair users
•LANDSCAPE•	Thames scenery, colourful houseboats, riverside pubs
•SUGGESTED MAP•	aqua3 OS Explorers 160 Windsor, Weybridge & Bracknell, 161 London South
•START•	Grid reference: TQ 093664
•FINISH•	Grid reference: TQ 152683
•DOG FRIENDLINESS•	Good, but do remember to scoop poop
•PARKING•	Behind Hampton Court Station at finish of walk
•PUBLIC TOILETS•	Cowey Sale (adjacent to Walton Bridge) and Molesey Lock
•NOTE•	Catch bus 451 or 461 to start, then walk back to car park

Walk 25 Directions

Cross the road in front of the station, and catch the bus to **Walton on Thames** from stop J, outside the Joshua Tree bar & brasserie.

The bus will drop you in **Hepworth Way**. Continue walking in the same direction, and follow the road round to the traffic lights. Cross over, and bear right into **Bridge Street**; then, just before the main span over the river, drop down the steps to your right, signposted '**Thames Path**'. (You can avoid the steps by turning left here, into **Walton Lane**; at the bottom of the slope, double back onto the **Thames Path** and continue under **Walton Bridge**.

At the foot of the steps turn left, then right, onto the riverside path. Climb over the ramped footbridge

at the entrance to **Walton Marina**; then, from here to the end of your walk, all you need to do is to keep the river on your left. There are no worries about route finding, so you're free to look around at the delights that the river has in store.

By now you're almost certain to have seen a few swans. This part of the river is an important place for them, for Sunbury is the starting point of the traditional annual census of 'Swan Upping'. In medieval times swan meat was an important part of any royal banquet, and all swans were

> **WHILE YOU'RE THERE** ⓘ
>
> Just across the river at the end of this walk, Hampton Court Palace needs no introduction. But for less than the cost of family ticket to the Palace you can pilot your own four-seater motor launch from **Hampton Ferry Hire Boats** for a pleasant couple of hours on the river.

Walk 25

WHERE TO EAT AND DRINK ⓘ
You'll be spoilt for choice! Along the route, the **Anglers** and the **Weir** are both large, riverside pubs with extensive menus and outside tables overlooking the water. A little further on, a short ferry ride to Hampton brings the **Bell**, the **White Hart** or the **Jolly Cooper's** within your grasp. At journey's end, you'll find Pizza Hut's **Streets of London** pub and the **Joshua Tree** bar & brasserie.

considered to be Crown property. Swan Upping also dates from this time, but although the colourful royal ceremonial still takes places each year in late July, the modern 'Uppers' are more concerned with ecology, conservation and animal welfare than with stocking Her Majesty's larder.

Sunbury Lock with its massive electrically operated gates is always a pleasant spot to watch the boats. Then, as the bustle of the lock slips behind, you'll be walking beside the low brick walls of **Molesey Reservoirs**. Beyond them, you'll pass a few houses set back from the water's edge before the river divides around **Platts Eyot**. The word eyot – pronounced like the alternative spelling 'ait' – derives from the Old English word ieg, and simply means a small island.

Next comes **Hurst Park**, now predominantly an area of 1970s period housing separated from the river by wide lawns. But the Hurst has a colourful sporting history; cricket and golf were both played here in the 18th century, and prize fights during the early 19th century attracted crowds of up to 10,000 people. For over 200 years, Hurst Park was also a popular horse racing venue, and the course was only closed as recently as 1962.

Across the river lies **Hampton**, with its sailing club and the prominent landmark of **St Mary's Church**. Hampton's vicars are known as far back as 1342 and, although the present building only dates from 1831, the triangle of streets around the church has been familiar since the early 16th century when Cardinal Wolsey began work on the great palace of **Hampton Court**. There's been a ferry here since that time, too, and it's still a delightful way of crossing the river to explore this historic area.

Just beyond the ferry lies **Garrick's Ait**. Behind it, on the Middlesex bank, the small domed building is **Garrick's Temple**, built in the mid-18th century by the actor David Garrick in honour of William Shakespeare. Then comes **Tagg's Island**, followed by the tree-lined section that leads you past Molesey Boat Club to Molesey Lock.

From the lock, the footpath runs briefly alongside **Hurst Road** to **Hampton Court Bridge**, just across the road from the car park at the end of your walk.

WHAT TO LOOK FOR ⓘ
Tagg's Island, connected to the Middlesex bank by a bridge, is now a popular houseboat mooring. Tom Tagg had a boatyard here in Victorian times, and he opened the Island Hotel in 1872. By the dawn of the last century business was slack, and in 1912 Fred Karno took over the lease. He demolished the building, and in its place constructed 'the finest and most luxurious river hotel in Europe'. But his timing was unfortunate; the First World War was imminent, and the initial popularity of his 'Karsino' was never repeated in the post war era. After several changes of name the building was demolished in 1971 to make way for a landscaped lagoon.

Walk 26

Chatley on Line

A varied walk to a unique 19th-century semaphore tower.

•DISTANCE•	5 miles (8km)
•MINIMUM TIME•	2hrs
•ASCENT / GRADIENT•	230ft (70m) ▲ ▲ ▲
•LEVEL OF DIFFICULTY•	👫 👫 👫
•PATHS•	Field edge paths and heathland tracks
•LANDSCAPE•	Arable farmland and wooded heath
•SUGGESTED MAP•	aqua3 OS Explorers 145 Guildford & Farnham, 146 Dorking, Box Hill & Reigate
•START / FINISH•	Grid reference: TQ 107594
•DOG FRIENDLINESS•	Livestock in some fields, also sections of minor road
•PARKING•	Downside Bridge, south of Cobham
•PUBLIC TOILETS•	None on route

Over the last decade, mobile phone masts have been sprinkled so thickly over the English landscape that we hardly notice them. But, hidden in the trees just yards from the growling M25 stands a communications tower quite unlike anything else you'll see. Built in 1822, Chatley Heath semaphore tower formed part of a line of hilltop stations used by the Royal Navy to signal messages between London and Portsmouth. The 13 stations were built at about 5 mile (8km) intervals and, because each one needed to be visible from its neighbours up and down the line, towers were constructed on the lower hills.

Mast-have Technology

Each building was individually designed to suit its location, but they all had one essential feature in common – a slotted mast with two hand-cranked semaphore arms, spelling out up to 48 different characters. On Chatley's low hill, 88 steps lead up to the roof of the five-storey tower, and the top of the mast is some 90ft (27m) from the ground. Almost two centuries ago, this was state of the art technology. Skilled operators could send up to six words a minute, and a complete message could be transmitted from the Admiralty to Portsmouth dockyard in around a quarter of an hour. Once a day, the system was cleared for the Navy's single most important piece of information – the one o'clock time signal.

Before modern satellite positioning, navigators depended on an accurate chronometer to calculate their ship's position. That's why the time signal acquired strategic importance – and why the Admiralty made such elaborate arrangements to transmit it. In 1833, a time ball was erected on the roof of the Royal Observatory at Greenwich. The ball was dropped at precisely 1PM each day and it took 12 seconds to relay the signal, by semaphore, to Portsmouth, and 11 seconds for the acknowledgement to return.

The system lasted until the end of December 1847, when the Admiralty began sending their signals over the London and Southampton Railway's new electric telegraph. The Chatley Heath tower was used as a house until 1963, and then fell derelict. In 1989 Surrey County Council restored the burnt out shell and opened it to the public. Now, you'll see displays explaining the history of semaphore, together with working models showing how the system was operated. The original winding gear and brass indicators have been installed on the top floor, and you can operate the semaphore arms to send a message of your own.

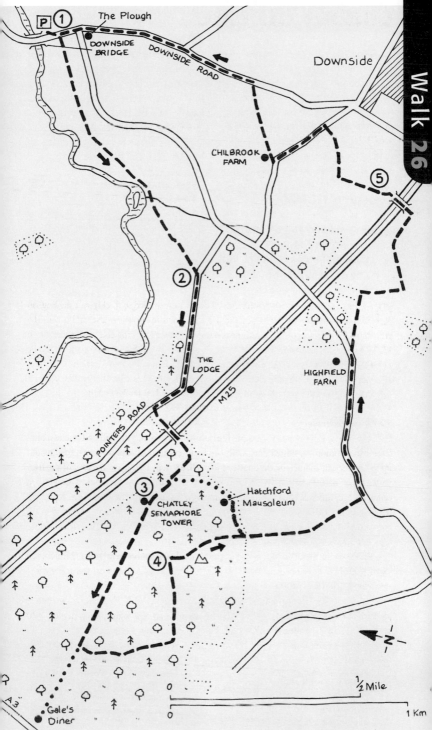

P ① The Plough
DOWNSIDE BRIDGE
DOWNSIDE ROAD
Downside
CHILBROOK FARM
⑤
②
THE LODGE
M25
POINTERS ROAD
HIGHFIELD FARM
③ CHATLEY SEMAPHORE TOWER
Hatchford Mausoleum
④
Gale's Diner
A3

½ Mile

1 Km

N

Walk 26

Walk 26 **Directions**

① Take the signposted footpath just across the road from the car park, and cross the fields to a small footbridge and stile. Nip over, and continue to the stile on the far side of the next field. Cross this one too, then follow the river bank to a footbridge close to some electricity lines. Beyond the bridge, take the signposted path across the fields towards **Pointers Road**.

② Turn right into **Pointers Road**, and continue for 130yds (119m) beyond the impressive wrought iron gates of **The Lodge**. Now turn left, cross the M25, and follow the tarmac lane as it winds up the hill to **Chatley semaphore tower**.

③ Pass the tower, and follow the waymarked route towards the **blue car park** until it dives between two bench seats into an area of dense fir trees. Turn left here, onto the broad sandy horse ride bordering the trees. Follow the ride as it crosses the route to the red car park, climbs to the top of a gentle hill, and veers around to the left. Continue for a further 350yds (320m) as far as the three-way wooden signpost.

④ Turn right and follow the bridleway to **Ockham Lane**. Turn left and continue along **Ockham Lane** until the road bears left at

Highfield Farm. Fork right onto the footpath to **Horsley Road**, and follow it over a stile as far as the three way signpost two-thirds of the way along the edge of a long, narrow field. Turn left here, across the field, towards **Chilbrook Farm Road**; walk through the gap in the far hedge, and follow the edge of the next field as far as the motorway bridge. Turn left over the M25.

WHAT TO LOOK FOR ⓘ

Not far from the semaphore tower, the **Hatchford Mausoleum** is an eerie and sad little building. This classical 'Temple of Sleep' was built by Sir Henry Samuelson in 1921 as a memorial to his father, Sir Bernard. The mausoleum initially contained a large copper table tomb, which had been moved from its original site at Torre Cemetery, Torquay. The tomb – which weighed almost a ton – was stolen in 1961, and nature is now slowly reclaiming the whole structure.

---

⑤ Just beyond the motorway, zig-zag left-right over a stile and follow the signposted route towards **Chilbrook Farm Lane**. At the far corner of the field, nip over the stile and bear right onto the waymarked farm road. Turn left into **Chilbrook Farm Lane**, then fork right at the pretty **Chilbrook Farm**. Go through the wicket gate, and take the signposted path towards **Downside Road**. At the far side of the field cross **Downside Road**, turn left, and follow the pavement back to the start of your walk.

WHILE YOU'RE THERE ⓘ

Cobham's **bus museum** features the largest collection of London buses in the world, with vehicles dating from 1925 to 1958. For something a bit faster, try the **Brooklands museum**, which includes part of the original banked motor racing circuit and buildings. There is also a fascinating aircraft collection.

WHERE TO EAT AND DRINK ⓘ

The 400 year old **Plough** has a traditional public bar and wood-panelled snug. Bar meals are only served at lunchtime – in the evening, you'll need to book at the pub's restaurant. Half way round the walk, a short diversion brings you to **Gale's Diner**, a little takeaway serving snacks and all day breakfasts.

Baynards' Railway Children

Explore the film locations for an early serialisation of Edith Nesbit's classic children's story.

•DISTANCE•	4¼ miles (7km)
•MINIMUM TIME•	2hrs
•ASCENT / GRADIENT•	98ft (30m)
•LEVEL OF DIFFICULTY•	
•PATHS•	Field and forest paths, section of old railway line
•LANDSCAPE•	Gently rolling farmland
•SUGGESTED MAP•	aqua3 OS Explorer 134 Crawley & Horsham
•START / FINISH•	Grid reference: TQ 078349
•DOG FRIENDLINESS•	Keep on lead near livestock
•PARKING•	Lay-by on Cox Green Road, Baynards, adjacent to railway bridge at start of walk
•PUBLIC TOILETS•	None on route

BACKGROUND TO THE WALK

> *'After quite a long search – walking on remote bits of line in the home counties and consulting ordnance maps, we have found a country station and a line that winds through a tunnel between high wooded hills…'*

Towards the end of a short feature in the Radio Times in March, 1957, the producer Dorothea Brooking recounted the difficulties of filming *The Railway Children* for BBC children's television. The country station that she found was Baynards, on the Guildford-to-Christ's Hospital line, where this walk begins, just a short way north of the tunnel that was used in the eight part serial.

Time Warp

Finding a suitable location for a story set in 1906 meant 'finding a station and a bit of line that is not electrified' – not that easy, even in 1957. Then, there was the practical problem of the 'modern trains running their day to day schedule'. Nearly half a century later, Carlton Television had an easier job with their 2000 remake of Edith Nesbit's classic children's story. Their film was shot on the preserved Bluebell Railway in Sussex, with a ready made set and turn of the century locomotives still in everyday use. Dorothea Brooking had no such luxury; in 1957, there wasn't a single standard gauge heritage railway operating anywhere in this country.

Twilight Years

Looking back at the classic Radio Times layout with its period advertisements, it's easy to imagine a comfortable, timeless era far removed from the social pressures and unremitting changes of our own age. But far from it. These were the twilight years for Britain's rural railways; traffic had collapsed after a strike in 1955 and, within a decade, the 'Beeching axe' would fall on hundreds of little stations like Baynards.

Action!

But Dorothea Brooking must have been coping with a different sort twilight. Filming took place in mid-February and the schedule allowed an extra day for the 'all too likely event of bad weather'. British Railways had arranged for a period engine and four carriages, and the train was filmed pulling into the station from the Guildford direction, stopping, and going on into the tunnel. There were also some shunting scenes in the station sidings.

The film starred Norman Shelley as the Old Gentleman and Anneke Willys, Sandra Michaels and Cavan Kendall played the children. They were shown exploring the station and goods shed, sitting on a piece of fence (provided by the BBC) and flagging down the train in the cutting. You'll see these film locations right at the start of your walk, though the tunnel itself is now blocked. There are good views of the station from the Downs Link – but please, do respect the owner's privacy.

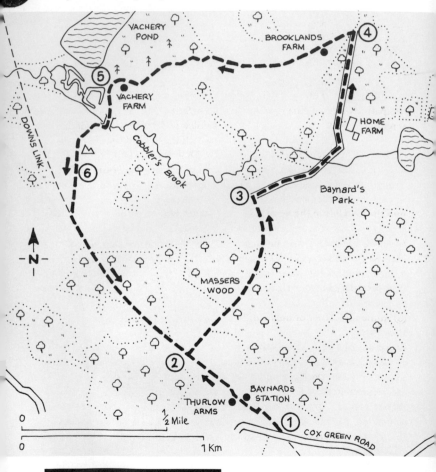

Walk 27 Directions

① From the lay-by, follow the **Downs Link** signposts down onto the old railway line and head north under the **Cox Green Road** bridge. Soon you'll come to a wooden gate as the old line approaches **Baynards Station**. Follow the **Downs Link** as it zig-zags left and right, past the station buildings, and back onto the

Walk 27

old line. There's a small picnic area here, an information panel, and the **Thurlow Arms** is on your left. Continue for 350yds (320m), until a footpath crosses the line at a waymarker post.

② Turn right here, nip over the stile, and cross the open field straight ahead. Keep just to the left of a corner of woodland jutting out into the field, jump the waymarked stile in front of you, and bear gently left along the grassy track through **Massers Wood**. Leave the woods at a waymarked stile, and follow the field boundary on your right.

③ At the top corner of the field, turn right over a stile onto the bridleway. Continue along the surfaced lane at the foot of the hill, towards the massive buildings of **Home Farm**. Follow the lane as it swings to the left past the farm, and continue for 80yds (73m) beyond the entrance to **Brooklands Farm** on your left.

④ Turn left here, onto a gravelled track that passes the back of the farm and continues as a grassy lane. At the end of the lane, carry on through two fields, following the edge of the woods on your right as

far as the buildings of **Vachery Farm**. Bear right here, and follow the signposted bridleway until it meets the farm drive at a fork.

⑤ Now bear left, signposted towards **Vachery Farm**; then, 20yds (18m) further on, fork right onto the signposted bridleway. Bear right through a small wood, cross the wooden footbridge over **Cobbler's Brook**, and go though a small gate. Now turn right, and follow the field edge as it bears around to the left and comes to a waymarked gate.

⑥ Go through the gate, and continue straight ahead along the waymarked bridleway. Follow it for 150yds (137m); then, as the bridleway bears to the left, dodge up to the right and turn left onto the **Downs Link**. Follow the old railway back to the **Thurlow Arms** and retrace your steps to the start.

The Mysterious Affair at Newlands Corner

The trail of an early 20th-century news story leads to a Surrey beauty spot.

•DISTANCE•	3 miles (4.8km)
•MINIMUM TIME•	1hr 30min
•ASCENT / GRADIENT•	442ft (135m) ▲▲▲
•LEVEL OF DIFFICULTY•	🚶🚶 🚶🚶 🚶
•PATHS•	Easy to follow tracks and paths
•LANDSCAPE•	Dramatic North Downs scenery
•SUGGESTED MAP•	aqua3 OS Explorer 145 Guildford & Farnham
•START / FINISH•	Grid reference: TQ 043492
•DOG FRIENDLINESS•	Some busy road crossings, watch out for dogs and cats at Timbercroft, and grazing cattle near Albury
•PARKING•	Newlands Corner
•PUBLIC TOILETS•	At car park

BACKGROUND TO THE WALK

In an extraordinary episode redolent of one of her own novels, Agatha Christie dominated the British papers during the first two weeks of December 1926. She never mentioned the affair in her autobiography, and the motive which fuelled 11 days of intense police and media activity has remained an enigma long after her death.

Agatha Miller married Colonel Archie Christie late in 1914. After wartime service in the Royal Flying Corps, Archie returned to civilian life when their daughter was born, five years later. Agatha's first novel was published in the following year and, by the mid '20s, income from her books helped the couple to buy their own home at Sunningdale in Berkshire.

Newlands Corner Mystery

But material success masked fault lines in the couple's relationship. The war years could not have been easy and, just possibly, Archie felt threatened by his wife's success. She put on weight after their daughter's birth, whilst he found consolation – and romance – on the golf course. On Friday, 3rd December 1926, there was a furious row as Archie told Agatha that he would be spending the weekend with his mistress, Nancy Neele. Divorce was inevitable.

That night, Agatha left her sleeping daughter and treasured dog, climbed into her bullnose Morris, and disappeared into the night. The following morning, the novelist's car was found abandoned by the chalk pit that you'll see in Water Lane, near the start of your walk. But Agatha Christie was gone. It was national news. Whilst the police scoured southern England and questioned Archie on suspected murder, the Daily News offered a £100 reward for information. The story remained in the press and, on Sunday 12th, thousands of people converged on Newlands Corner to search for Agatha's body. Meanwhile, almost 24 hours after her disappearance, Agatha Christie had calmly booked into a Harrogate hotel under the assumed name of Teresa Neele. Despite the national hue and cry, ten days elapsed before the police located her. Archie was in the clear, deflecting reporters by explaining his wife had amnesia, and the couple fled to Abney Hall in Cheshire, home of Agatha's sister.

This bizarre affair has been shrouded in mystery ever since. Christie herself refused even to discuss it and, after her death, there were unsuccessful attempts to suppress a film adaptation of the story. The unsolved mystery was featured on BBC television in 1997, and the programme included an appearance by author Jared Cade. His subsequent book claims that the entire episode was simply Christie's attempt to embarrass her husband and sabotage his weekend with his mistress. It is, at least, a convincing theory.

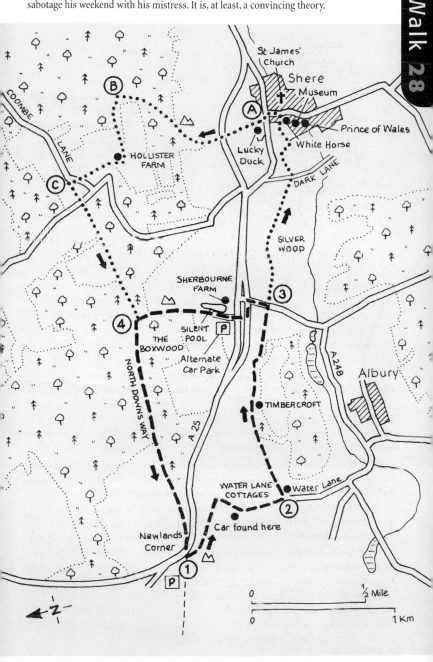

Walk 28

Walk 28 Directions

① Walk back from the car park towards the main road and, 50yds (46m) from the entrance, turn right onto the waymarked byway. To begin with there are fine views across the Weald, but soon the track drops into the trees and comes to a junction at an old Second World War pill box. Swing right here, and follow the byway as it bears left past the **old chalk pit** where Agatha Christie's car was abandoned in December 1926. Look out for a turning on your right, then carry straight on for a further 200yds (183m).

WHAT TO LOOK FOR

Many legends surround the tree-shaded **Silent Pool**, close by Sherbourne Farm. Even in high summer you'll feel a slight chill in the air, and there's something rather unearthly about its clear, bluish-green water. Believe, if you will, that a young maiden was taking her customary dip when the wicked King John rode into the water to carry her off. Despite her brother's efforts to save her, both brother and sister perished, 'locked in each other's arms in the tranquil crystal depth'. It's said that on moonlit nights a white form bathes here still, until with a hideous shriek it disappears below the dark surface.

② Turn left onto the unmarked bridleway, passing **Water Lane Cottages** on your right. Continue to the fork at **Timbercroft**, and bear right onto the footpath towards the **Silent Pool**. There are dogs and cats living here, so it's best to have your own dog on a lead. Fork right again after 100yds (91m), onto the narrow, signposted public footpath. Take care as you cross the quarry access road, then continue as far as the A248.

③ Cross over, turn left onto the footpath which runs just inside the hedge, and walk up to the A25. Turn left at the top, re-cross the A248, then follow the A25 footpath for 100yds (91m). Now cross the busy main road and join the footpath, up past **Sherbourne Farm**. Just beyond the farm entrance, your waymarked path is crossed by the broad, gravelled track leading up from the car park. Fork right here to visit **Sherbourne Pond** and the **Silent Pool**.

WHERE TO EAT AND DRINK

The all-year-round kiosk in **Newlands Corner** car park sells hot and cold drinks and snacks, including burgers, chips, soup, salad rolls and cakes.

Return to the narrow, waymarked path to continue your walk. The path climbs gently at first, then plunges into the **Boxwood** and begins the serious assault on the Downs. It eases off towards the top, and meets the **North Downs Way National Trail** at an acorn waymark.

④ Turn left onto the **North Downs Way**, then keep right 300yds (274m) further on, as another track forks off down the hill. Now you can settle into your stride for a mile (1.6km) of level walking back to the busy A25, bang opposite the **car park** where your walk began.

WHILE YOU'RE THERE

If you're interested in animals, farming or wildlife, then you'll enjoy a visit to **Sherbourne Farm**, adjacent to the Silent Pool on Shere Road. It's no theme park, but a family run working farm where you can see seasonal displays ranging from lambing, shearing and calving to planting and harvesting. Children especially enjoy feeding the hens, ducks and geese.

The Shere Loop

Extend your walk to the bustling little village of Shere, or park at the Silent Pool and make this a completely independent route.
See map and information panel for Walk 28

•DISTANCE•	5½ miles (9km) or 3½ (5.7km) if starting from Silent Pool
•MINIMUM TIME•	2hrs
•ASCENT / GRADIENT•	541ft (165m) ▲▲▲
•LEVEL OF DIFFICULTY•	林 林 林

Walk 29 Directions (Walk 28 option)

Leave the main route at Point ③, cross the A248, and take the footpath directly opposite. Nip over the stile, then continue across an open field and into **Silver Wood**. The path climbs briefly, then glides down the sandy woodland path. Leave the woods at a small metal gate, walk straight across the next field, and cross **Dark Lane**.

Now follow the path beside an old brick wall, and turn right at the **Old Rectory**. Drop down past the ford, and follow the lane beside the stream towards **Shere** village. Huddled around its diminutive square (Point ④), Shere is as pretty a place as you could hope to find. There's a whole range of shops and services here, not to mention the public toilets, converted from the restored 1885 Voluntary Fire Station in Middle Street.

Turn left into **Middle Street**, then left again into **Upper Street**. A few paces further on, turn right at the **Manor House**, and follow the signposted byway that climbs serenely under the A25 and winds past a wartime pill box before levelling out and coming to a crossroads with the **North Downs Way**. You'll see a big circular tank on your left here, as well as the acorn waymarks (Point Ⓑ).

Turn left, and enjoy a section of fast, level walking to **Hollister Farm**. Just beyond the farm the track swings to the right and there are two forks within the next 200yds (183m). Keep right at both of them, continuing down the narrower path as far as **Combe Lane** (Point Ⓒ). Turn right here; then, a few paces further on, swing off to the left along the **North Downs Way**. Cross **Staple Lane**, and continue along the level, waymarked trail to rejoin the main route at Point ④.

> **WHAT TO LOOK FOR** ⓘ
> At St James' Church in Shere look for two small openings in the north wall of the chancel, and a sealed off archway on the outside of the same wall. These are all that remain of a tiny cell. In 1329, Christine Carpenter was given permission to be enclosed in this cell, where she could see the altar and receive Communion through the holes. She came out briefly in 1332, but was soon 'thrust back into the said re-enclosure' on the Bishop's orders, to learn 'how nefarious was her committed sin'.

Runnymede: the Last Salute

An easy to follow route across historic meadowland spanning eight centuries of freedom and democracy.

•DISTANCE•	3 miles (4.8km)
•MINIMUM TIME•	1hr 30min
•ASCENT / GRADIENT•	213ft (65m) ▲▲ ▲▲
•LEVEL OF DIFFICULTY•	👫 👫 👫
•PATHS•	Woodland and cross-field paths, boggy in wet weather
•LANDSCAPE•	Wooded slopes overlooking Thames-side meadowlands
•SUGGESTED MAP•	aqua3 OS Explorer 160 Windsor, Weybridge & Bracknell or National Trust's trail map, (available at tea room)
•START / FINISH•	Grid reference: SU 996731
•DOG FRIENDLINESS•	Not permitted in paddock behind National Trust tea room, or in Air Forces Memorial
•PARKING•	National Trust car park, Runnymede
•PUBLIC TOILETS•	At car park

Walk 30 Directions

This walk makes use of the National Trust's superbly waymarked trails, and includes an extra stretch across the meadows to the east before returning along the Thames Path. You'll pass the John F Kennedy memorial, as well as two very different monuments designed by Sir Edward Maufe, architect of Guildford cathedral.

From the **information board** at the car park entrance, follow the waymarked purple route across the field to your right. At the edge of the woods, a short diversion leads you through a little gate and up the cobbled steps to the **Kennedy memorial**. Take care in wet weather, when the granite setts can be treacherous.

Return to the gate and turn right. A short way further on, you'll see the **American Bar Association**

Memorial, also on your right. Constructed in 1957, this simple yet effective little building is dedicated to Magna Carta's principles of freedom, enshrined in these fields in 1215.

A few paces further on turn right over the stile, then bear left, and follow the marker posts beside a line of oak trees until you reach a wicket gate in the woods straight ahead. Turn right here, following

---

WHAT TO LOOK FOR ⓘ

You're almost certain to see and hear sizeable flocks of **Canada geese** honking in the meadows surrounding Langham Ponds. These large, noisy birds have unmistakable long black necks and heads, with a bold white flash extending around the cheeks and under the chin. Like swans, Canada geese pair for life, and may live for as long as 20 years. They were first brought to this country from the American colonies in the 17th century, to decorate the landscaped parks of the gentry.

Walk 30

WHERE TO EAT AND DRINK ⓘ
You'll get a warm welcome at the **National Trust tea room** at the start, which also sells maps, guide books and souvenirs. The full menu includes hot and cold drinks, all day breakfasts, light lunches, sandwiches, cakes and cream teas, as well as hot daily specials like pasta bake or cottage pie. Open daily, except 24–26 December.

the purple route up the steps towards the **Air Forces Memorial**. At the top of the steps, turn right to walk along the gravelled road and continue around to the right to the memorial entrance.

The scene that confronts you is surprisingly awesome in its scale. Beyond the immaculately tended gardens stands a huge white Portland stone building, opened by the Queen in October 1953. It overlooks the meadows where the Archbishop of Canterbury, Stephan Langton, and his baronial followers forced the King to recognise English freedoms in Magna Carta, and its walls record the names of over 20,000 Commonwealth aircrew who died for those same ideals during the Second World War, but whose bones have no known grave.

You don't need to have lost a loved one in the war, or even to have lived through it, to be humbled by this place. Three hundred panels stand in the cloistered quadrangle, arranged beside the tall window embrasures like pages from an open book. Each one bears over 60 names, grouped according to the year in which they died. There's a small shrine beneath the tower and, before you leave, you can lighten the mood by climbing the spiral stairs to the roof for a view over London and six counties.

Retrace your route past the **Royal Holloway College** and down the steps to the first waymark post. Turn right here, and follow the waymarked woodland path down the hill to a yellow and purple waymark. Turn right again, now following the yellow trail just inside the woodland edge until it veers to the left through a little wicket gate. Bear right at **Langham Pond**, jump the stile, and follow the water's edge until you come to a yellow waymark by another wicket gate.

Keep straight on here, beside the post and wire fence on your left, and turn left through the next wicket gate. Continue along the waymarked path towards the buildings on the horizon, following the hedge line as it loops all the way around to the left to a field gate with a wicket gate beside it.

Go through here, and follow the waymarked footpath straight across the open meadow in front of you. At the far side, two stiles in quick succession lead you to another wicket gate; cross the road here, and turn left onto the **Thames Path** at a yellow waymark post. Now, simply follow the river all the way back to the car park and tea room where your walk began.

WHILE YOU'RE THERE ⓘ
Splash out on a **boat trip** to complete your day on the River Thames. In the summer months, the replica Victorian paddler *Lucy Fisher* runs regular 45-minute trips from Runnymede landing stage, adjacent to the start of your walk. There are longer cruises through Old Windsor Lock on Sunday afternoons, as well as regular services to Hampton Court and Windsor. You can buy refreshments on board, and all the boats have toilets.

Walk 31

With the Romans and Celts at Farley

A secluded walk through 2,000 years of history on the Greensand ridge.

•DISTANCE•	5 miles (8km)
•MINIMUM TIME•	2hrs 30min
•ASCENT / GRADIENT•	574ft (175m) ▲▲▲
•LEVEL OF DIFFICULTY•	🚶 🚶 🚶
•PATHS•	Forest tracks and rutted lanes, running in water after rain
•LANDSCAPE•	Remote wooded hillsides, occasional farms and cottages
•SUGGESTED MAP•	aqua3 OS Explorer 145 Guildford & Farnham
•START / FINISH•	Grid reference: TQ 051448
•DOG FRIENDLINESS•	Can mainly run free, on lead on roadside section
•PARKING•	Forest car park (number 8) on Farley Heath
•PUBLIC TOILETS•	None on route

BACKGROUND TO THE WALK

High on windswept Farley Heath, you're standing close to the remains of a Romano-Celtic temple, one of the few Roman sites to have been found in Surrey. In Roman times, you'd have got here along the branch road that led north west from Stane Street – the busy London to Chichester highway – at present day Rowhook, on the outskirts of Horsham. You'll cross the line of the road near Winterfold Cottage, and again on Ride Lane, just after the junction with Madgehole Lane.

Pick 'n' Mix Religion

The Romans had a plethora of religious beliefs. They venerated Rome and the Emperor, as well as Jupiter and other Graeco-Roman gods; in far flung outposts like Britain they also embraced the local and pagan religions. By the 3rd and 4th centuries Christianity was gaining ground, and there was increasing interest in mystical religions like the cult of Mithras, the ancient Persian light god.

Both Roman and native gods were worshipped together in Britain, and distinctive Romano-Celtic temples were evolved to accommodate the various different religions. These designs consisted of a square or rectangular tower surrounded by a lean-to verandah, and they were quite unlike other buildings in the Roman landscape.

Uncovering the Past

Farley was typical, and you can see the outline of its foundations just a few paces north of the car park at the start of your walk. The two concentric masonry squares are a modern reconstruction, built to show the ground plan that was discovered by Martin Tupper in 1848, and confirmed by subsequent excavations in 1939 and 1995. The temple itself was built before the end of the 1st century AD. It was enclosed within a precinct wall, or *temenos*, which was also located during the excavations but has since been re-buried. Tupper's finds, which included several decorated bronze strips from a priest's sceptre, are now in the British Museum.

The temple was fairly isolated, although there was a Roman villa just south of Pitch Hill, some 3 miles (5km) back down the road towards Stane Street. No other permanent buildings have been found inside the temple precincts, but the site would have been the focus of regular religious rites, and possibly occasional markets or fairs as well. The temple remained in use until the end of the Roman occupation early in the 5th century, and it seems that the building burnt down some time before the year 450.

Walk 31 Directions

① Stand in the car park facing the road and walk to the entrance on your right-hand side. Cross the road, and follow the signposted public bridleway across **Farley Heath**. Keep to the right at the first fork, and continue straight across when you get to the the sandy bridleway crossroads.

Keep straight on again at the five-way junction, and take the fork to the right a few paces further on. Then, as the main track swings round hard to the left, continue down the waymarked woodland footpath straight ahead. You'll wind gently down to a waymark post; turn right here, and follow the public bridleway for a further 70yds (64m) to a T-junction with **Madgehole Lane**.

② Turn right and follow this deeply rutted, sunken lane until it meets a narrow tarmac road at a pretty, tile hung cottage.

③ Turn left, signposted towards **Winterfold**, and climb through this delightful, sequestered valley past the rambling, half-timbered **Madgehole Farm** to **Madgehole**. Here you leave the tarmac and swing hard right, climbing steadily past a young Christmas tree plantation on your left. Follow the waymarked bridleway as it winds right, then left, through **Great Copse**, and join the **Greensand Way** as it swings in from your right.

WHERE TO EAT AND DRINK

You won't find any refreshment stops on this route, so I'd recommend that you pack a drink and a chocolate bar at the very least. After your walk, follow the road towards Shere. Just beyond the railway bridge you'll come to the pink-washed **William IV** at Little London, a 16th-century free house with flagstone floors and a huge inglenook fireplace. They serve good home cooked food (though not on Sunday evenings) together with a decent range of real ales.

④ Turn left onto **Row Lane** and, after 150yds (137m), fork right towards Ewhurst and Shere. Follow the road over the brow of the hill, until you come to car park 5 on your right. Turn left here, onto an unsignposted footpath into the woods, and keep right at the fork 90yds (82m) further on. Almost at once, bear left off the main track, up a narrow footpath by the side of a wire fence. This leads you down beside the huge garden of **Winterfold Cottage**, to another waymarker post. Fork left here, and follow the public bridleway along the rough cottage drive until you reach **Row Lane**.

WHILE YOU'RE THERE

After seeing the temple, you might be curious to know what a Roman priest's headdress looked like. Well, you can see one in **Guildford museum**. Right next to the Castle Arch in Quarry Street, you'll find Surrey's largest collection of archaeology and local history; everything from Palaeolithic hand axes to a super collection of 17th-century pottery and glass. The needlework displays include samplers, patchwork and baby clothes, and the museum also features pictures and artefacts illustrating most aspects of local life. The museum is open Monday to Saturday, and admission is free.

⑤ Cross over and continue along the bridleway. After 200yds (183m) it bears hard right onto **Ride Lane**, which will carry you all the way to **Farley Green**. Keep right at the junction with **Madgehole Lane**, and trudge steadily through this rutted, prehistoric landscape until gradually the banks roll back as you approach **Farley Green Hall Farm**.

⑥ Pass the lovely old half-timbered farmhouse on your right, and keep bearing left until you come to the top of the green. Bear left again, and follow **Farley Heath Road** for the final stretch back to your car.

WHAT TO LOOK FOR

I saw dozens of **rooks** foraging in the fields as I tramped down Ride Lane towards Farley Green. Rooks return to established breeding sites year after year, building their large, sprawling nests in tall trees such as beech or oak. It's not unusual to find 50 or more nests in a single rookery. There's an old saying that, if you see two crows, then they're actually rooks. The crow always seems to be a much more solitary bird than the noisy, gregarious rook. If you want to be certain of telling these large black birds apart, then look for the rook's conspicuous bare cheeks at the base of the bill.

Pyrford's Romantic Runaways

A charming circuit that follows the peaceful River Wey for much of the route.

•DISTANCE•	3½ miles (5.7km)
•MINIMUM TIME•	1hr 30min
•ASCENT / GRADIENT•	Negligible
•LEVEL OF DIFFICULTY•	
•PATHS•	Riverside tow path, some field paths and roadside
•LANDSCAPE•	Flat river valley with extensive water-meadows
•SUGGESTED MAP•	aqua3 OS Explorer 145 Guildford & Farnham
•START / FINISH•	Grid reference: TQ 039573
•DOG FRIENDLINESS•	Mostly run free but on lead for roadside and golf course
•PARKING•	Unsurfaced car park at start
•PUBLIC TOILETS•	None on route

BACKGROUND TO THE WALK

You could hardly imagine a more romantic hideaway than Queen Elizabeth's summerhouse. This mellow, red brick building stands two storeys high, with a first floor entrance and a curious, ogee-pitched roof to keep off the rain. At just fourteen feet square you wouldn't hold a party here, but it's a cosy enough little spot for two; you'll see it on the riverbank in the grounds of Pyrford Place, half a mile south of Pyrford Lock. A blue plaque on the wall records that the poet and clergyman John Donne lived here in the early years of the 17th century – but that isn't the half of it…

Forbidden Love

John Donne was born into a wealthy London family in 1572. He was educated at Oxford and Cambridge, and went on to study law and theology at the Inns of Court in London. It's clear that Donne was a deeply religious young man, yet he was also passionate by nature; he had inherited a considerable fortune and he spent his money on womanising, on books, and on all the pleasures that London could offer.

After his studies, Donne passed a couple of years with naval adventures to Spain and the Azores, before returning to London in 1598 to begin a promising career as secretary to Sir Thomas Egerton, Keeper of the Great Seal. In the same year he met the love of his life, Egerton's 14 year-old niece, Anne More. The couple married secretly in 1601, when Anne was just 17. John was in trouble, big time. Anne's father, Sir George More, had him thrown into the Fleet Prison, together with two friends who had helped to conceal the affair. Although Sir George later relented and allowed the marriage to stand, the episode had cost John his job; his own money had gone and, with a growing family to support, things were looking bleak.

Thicker Than Water

Luckily for the two lovers, not all of Anne's family were so prickly. Her cousin offered them shelter at Pyrford Place, where they spent the early years of their married life. John began to earn a small income from legal work; Anne's father was reconciled and paid his daughter's dowry; and John entered the church, becoming royal chaplain in 1615. But then, just as things were starting to improve, tragedy struck. In 1617, Anne died after giving birth to the couple's twelfth child, which was stillborn. She was only 33. John was devastated. He continued to write poetry, but sermons now took the place of love songs. In 1621 James I appointed him Dean of St Paul's, and he held the post until his death ten years later.

Walk 32 **Directions**

① Walk through the car park, cross the bridge at the traffic lights, and follow the roadside pavement towards **Pyrford** village. The pavement begins on the right-hand side and crosses the water-meadows on several small bridges. There are good views of **Newark Priory** here and, in wet weather, the flooded

fields attract swans and other water fowl. Now the pavement switches to the left hand side, and you cross the Bourne stream bridge; then, as the road swings hard right at **Church Hill**, keep straight on up the steep woodland path to **St Nicholas Church**.

② Bear right past the church, cross the road, and take the stone-flagged path through the churchyard. Nip

WHERE TO EAT AND DRINK ⓘ

The riverside conservatory and patio at the **Anchor** are popular spots to sit and watch the boats moving up and down through Pyrford lock. You might not fall in love with the architecture of this large, 1930s building, but so what? It's a handy halfway stop, there's a friendly welcome, and you can get something to eat here at any time of day. Choose from a nice selection of sensibly priced bar snacks and meals, plus a traditional roast on Sundays.

WHAT TO LOOK FOR ⓘ

This walk abounds in romance, and the forlorn remains of **Newark Priory** are as romantic as any Victorian watercolour. The Priory was probably founded by Augustinian Canons late in the 12th century. It would have been abandoned at the Dissolution in 1536, so the buildings were almost certainly falling into ruins by the time that John Donne knew them. The flint walls of the presbytery and the south transept still stand almost to their original height – but take your binoculars for a closer look, as the ruins are on private land.

over the two stiles at the far side and follow the signposted path past **Lady Place**. Bear left under the first set of power lines, following the field edge on your right. Carry straight on past the footpath turnings, right and left, as you approach a second set of power lines; cross two stiles, and continue for 60yds (55m) to a public footpath signpost directly under the wires. Turn right and head towards the corner of a garden that juts out into the field. Bear slightly left here, keeping the fence on your left hand side. Continue over a stile at **Pyrford Green House** and down the gravelled drive to **Warren Lane**.

WHILE YOU'RE THERE ⓘ

Whatever the season, you're sure to enjoy the colourful displays at the Royal Horticultural Society's world famous **Wisley gardens**. As well as the collections of flowers, alpines, fruit and vegetables, you'll see a variety of demonstration gardens packed with practical ideas that will keep you busy long after you get home. With its restaurant, gift shop and plant centre, Wisley has something for everyone. The gardens are open all year round, but you won't get in on Sundays unless you're an RHS member.

③ Zig-zag right and left across the road, then take the signposted

public footpath up the side of an open field. Carry on over the small footbridge straight ahead and follow the waymarked route across **Pyrford Golf Course**. This is an attractive place, but don't let that distract you from the golfers and the threat presented by their flying golf balls. You'll come out onto **Lock Lane**, just by **Pyrford Lock**. Turn right here and walk across the bridge by the **Anchor pub**.

④ Turn right again, to join the easy-to-follow **River Wey** tow path. Just past **Walsham Lock**, the tow path zig-zags left and right across the weir, and you continue walking with the river on your right. Cross the little footbridge at **Newark Lock**, where you'll get the best views of the remains of **Newark Priory**. From here continue along the tow path; you're now on the north side of the river. Beyond the lock, you'll come to **Newark Lane**; take a left turn here, and cross over **Newark Bridge** to return to the car park where your walk began.

Guildford Through the Looking Glass

A literary walk that takes in some delightfully varied sections of Guildford's local countryside.

•DISTANCE•	4 ¼ miles (7km)
•MINIMUM TIME•	2hrs
•ASCENT / GRADIENT•	344ft (105m) ▲▲▲
•LEVEL OF DIFFICULTY•	🚶🚶 🚶🚶 🚶🚶
•PATHS•	Paved streets, downland tracks and riverside tow path
•LANDSCAPE•	Big views from Pewley Down and gentle riparian scenery
•SUGGESTED MAP•	aqua3 OS Explorer 145 Guildford & Farnham
•START / FINISH•	Grid reference: SU 991494
•DOG FRIENDLINESS•	Town streets and tow path, so don't forget to scoop poop!
•PARKING•	Farnham Road car park, next to Guildford railway station
•PUBLIC TOILETS•	At car park

BACKGROUND TO THE WALK

As a small boy, I well remember my parents reading to me from a large, dark blue edition of *Alice in Wonderland*. Although the book's flyleaf was autographed by Lewis Carroll, it wasn't much of a collector's item. The signature was genuine enough, but the writing belonged to a friend of my father's – a man whose name really was Lewis Carroll.

A Rector's Son

By contrast, the famous children's author entered this life in 1832 with the name of Charles Dodgson. The eldest son of a Cheshire rector, Charles studied mathematics at Oxford, where he later became a university lecturer. Meanwhile the family had moved to Yorkshire and, after his father's death in 1868, his sisters set their hearts on moving to Guildford.

Charles bought them 'The Chestnuts', a large house in Castle Hill that you'll see on your way out of town; he spent a good deal of his own time there, too, and came to regard the place as home. He stayed at The Chestnuts every Christmas, and it was in Guildford that he began work on *The Hunting of the Snark*.

But Dodgson's job was in Oxford, where he was often surrounded by his colleague's young children. He wrote them countless letters, frequently including fantastic tales illustrated with his own sketches. He was a great story teller, too, gifted at weaving everyday events into elaborate fables whilst the children listened at his knee.

One of those children was Alice Liddell, daughter of the Dean of Christ Church. She was just four years old when her family moved to Oxford and, with her brother and two sisters, she delighted in Dodgson's company. They would go on walks and picnics together and, of course, he would tell them stories. But Alice was different; not content with just hearing her stories, she begged the mathematics lecturer to write them down for her.

And so, after a day out picnicking with the children on the Thames in 1862, Charles Dodgson sat down to write the manuscript of *Alice in Wonderland*. His friends eventually persuaded him to get the story published; but, when the book finally appeared with its well-known Tenniel illustrations, Dodgson's name was nowhere to be seen. Even the author, Lewis Carroll, was a creature of his own imagination.

When I was in my late teens, my father introduced me to his friend who was also called Lewis Carroll. We spent many happy Sunday mornings visiting his Surrey home. Like his literary namesake, this Lewis lived in a strange fantasy world, and our time there was regulated by a wall clock which struck the hour once every 30 minutes. But that, I'm afraid, is another story altogether…

Walk 33

Walk 33 Directions

① Leave the car park via the footbridge at Level 5, cross **Farnham Road**, and turn right. Just beyond the railway bridge drop into the subway on your left, and follow the signposts to the 'Town Centre via Riverside Walk'. Follow the riverside walk to the **White House** pub. Turn left over the bridge, continue into **High Street**, and turn first right into **Quarry Street**. Pass **Guildford Museum** and turn immediately left through **Castle Arch**. Your route forks right here, into **Castle Hill**, but a quick diversion up the pedestrian path straight ahead brings you to the *Looking Glass* statue in the small garden through an iron gateway on

> **WHILE YOU'RE THERE** ℹ️
> Don't leave Guildford without making a trip to **Dapdune Wharf**, formerly the barge building site for the River Wey Navigation and now the National Trust's visitor centre. Here you'll find the restored Wey barge *Reliance*, together with interactive displays telling the story of one of the oldest river navigations in the country.

your right. Retrace your steps, and follow **Castle Hill** past **The Chestnuts**. Turn left at the top, walk down **South Hill**, and turn right into **Pewley Hill**. Climb steadily past the **Semaphore House** on the corner of **Semaphore Road**; this was the next station down the line from Chatley Heath (➤ Walk 26). At the end of the road, continue

> **WHERE TO EAT AND DRINK** ℹ️
> Guildford's lively centre will spoil you for choice. Relax in the **King's Head's** flower filled courtyard or try **Scruffy Murphy's**, the **White House** or the **George Abbot** all overlooking the river.

along the bridleway and follow it to the striking viewpoint pillar on the summit of **Pewley Down**.

② Fork right at the viewpoint and follow the path off the ridge, keeping the hedge on your left. Soon you'll enter a tunnel of trees, and emerge between hedges. Keep straight on at the crossroads by the **Pewley Down** information board, and continue for 300yds (274m) until the path bears right and meets the **North Downs Way** National Trail at an acorn waymark post.

> **WHAT TO LOOK FOR** ℹ️
> In Castle Gardens look out for the statue of *Alice Through the Looking Glass* by Jean Argent. On the other side of the river, Edwin Russell's Alice listens as her sister reads her a story; while the White Rabbit darts down a nearby rabbit hole.

③ Turn right here and follow the waymarked **North Downs Way** past **South Warren Farm** to the residential street called **Pilgrims Way**. Turn left and follow the road past the junction with **Clifford Manor Road**.

④ Continue along **Pilgrims Way** to the A281. Cross over and walk across **Shalford Park**, signposted towards Godalming and Shalford. Beyond the trees you'll reach the **River Wey**; cross the footbridge, and follow the tow path towards **Guildford**, with the river on your right. Cross the lattice girder footbridge at **Millmead Lock**, and continue past the *Alice* statue on the little green near the **White House** pub. Now, just follow the riverbank until you reach the prominent **1913 Electricity Work**s on the opposite bank. Turn left, climb the steps, and retrace your outward route through the subway to the car park.

St Martha's Loop

A longer circuit to one of Surrey's oldest and most memorable churches.
See map and information panel for Walk 33

Walk 34

•DISTANCE•	6 miles (9.7km)
•MINIMUM TIME•	2hrs 30min
•ASCENT / GRADIENT•	738ft (225m) ▲▲▲
•LEVEL OF DIFFICULTY•	🚶🚶🚶 🚶

Walk 34 Directions (Walk 33 option)

To visit the **Church of St Martha**, leave the main route at Point ③, and turn left onto the **North Downs Way**. Follow the waymarked route across **Halfpenny Lane**, and climb the sandy track to **St Martha's Church** on the summit of **St Martha's Hill** (Point Ⓐ).

Turn right at the church, and take the footpath leading out of the churchyard directly opposite the south transept. You'll drop steeply down to **Chilworth Manor**, where you turn right at the bottom of the hill; a short way further on, turn left onto the manor house drive. Follow the drive out to a bend in **Halfpenny Lane**, and keep straight on to the sharp left hand bend at **Halfpenny Corner** (Point Ⓑ).

Continue straight ahead for just a few paces, then fork right up the unsignposted path between the hedges bordering two large houses. You'll come out briefly onto **Halfpenny Lane**; turn left, then left again at the public footpath sign a few paces further on. Go through the gate, and follow the field edge path on your left (Point Ⓒ).

Continue past a range of red roofed barns to **Manor Farm**. Here the path zig-zags to the right and to the left, and you continue with a hedge on your left and an open field on your right. When the hedge comes to an end, veer to the right and follow the path across the open field. Look just to the right as you go, for a tantalising glimpse of Guildford's distinctively modern cathedral in the distance (Point Ⓓ).

On the far side of the field you'll come to a stile. Nip across, then turn right onto **Clifford Manor Road**. Follow it around to the left and out onto **Pilgrims Way**, where you rejoin the main route by turning left at Point ④.

WHAT TO LOOK FOR ⓘ

The isolated little Norman **Church of St Martha** stands on the Pilgrim's Way, about ½ mile (800m) from the nearest road. There's been a church here for more than 1,000 years, though the building you'll see now was extensively restored by Henry Woodyer in 1846–50, following one of the alarmingly frequent explosions at Chilworth gunpowder mills at the foot of the hill. The little cruciform building, which looks for all the world like a miniature-sized cathedral, is still used for regular Sunday worship. It is normally open to visitors at weekends and bank holidays.

Walk 35

Linking the Downs at Bramley

There's plenty of interest along this easily followed old railway trail.

•DISTANCE•	4¾ miles (7.7km)
•MINIMUM TIME•	2hrs
•ASCENT / GRADIENT•	82ft (25m)
•LEVEL OF DIFFICULTY•	
•PATHS•	Bridleway following railway track, can be muddy after rain
•LANDSCAPE•	Gentle, well wooded river valley
•SUGGESTED MAP•	aqua3 OS Explorers 134 Crawley & Horsham, 145 Guildford & Farnham
•START•	Grid reference: TQ 010451
•FINISH•	Grid reference: TQ 055391
•DOG FRIENDLINESS•	A great walk, but scoop the poop or pay the fine!
•PARKING•	Stocklund Square car park, entrance off High Street
•PUBLIC TOILETS•	Cranleigh's leisure centre car park
•NOTE•	Park at end of walk, then catch bus 53 or 63 to Bramley

Walk 35 Directions

Walk back out of the car park, turn right, and catch bus 53 or 63 to **Bramley** from the bus shelter just in front of the large public clock in **Stocklund Square**.

The bus will drop you 100yds (91m) short of the former level crossing, so continue in the same direction until you reach the wooden gate onto the old trackbed. The line has now been converted into a bridleway, and the **Downs Link** and the **Wey South Path** both share the route here.

Take a look at the old station across the road to your right, before turning left to begin your walk along the old track. The low, wooded embankment eases its way south out of Bramley, and domestic gardens nuzzle the railway banks.

Even today, local people still recount how a train was machine gunned by a German fighter plane on this section during the Second World War; luckily, however, the only casualties were a couple of people injured by flying glass.

> **WHERE TO EAT AND DRINK** ⓘ
> Cranleigh claims to be England's largest village but is really a small town. In the High Street you'll find both **ASK Pizza** and **Pizza Express**, and the **Onslow Arms**. For lunches my own favourite is **Tiffins Tea Room** (opposite the war memorial) although, like **Sea Fare** fish and chips, it's closed on Sundays.

The line was originally promoted by the independent Horsham and Guildford Direct Railway Company, but was taken over by the powerful London, Brighton & South Coast Railway after the original contractor went bankrupt. The Brighton company completed the project –

and promptly hit a snag which delayed the line's opening until October 1865.

Just across the Sussex border, the track through Rudgwick station was on a steep slope, and the Railway Inspector insisted that the gradient should be eased before trains could start running. This meant raising the embankments south of the station, and building a new girder bridge directly above the original brick arch over the River Arun. The two bridges remain one on top of the other to this day, and are now immortalised in the logo for the Downs Link path.

WHAT TO LOOK FOR ⓘ

Your walk begins at Bramley and Wonersh station and, although the station buildings are long gone, it's still an interesting landmark on the route. You'll see the platforms, as well as two of the station name boards. These were taken down when the line was closed in 1965, but the Parish Council rediscovered them 30 years later and put them back. The wall mounted postbox, which is still in use, is built into the remains of the station master's house.

As the track pulls clear of **Bramley**, look out for an open field on your left. The old **Wey and Arun Canal** runs in the trees on the far side of the field, and soon you'll see it at the foot of the embankment on your left. The two old rivals run side by side for a time, until the railway enters a cutting and the last of the road noise dies away.

A little further on, a track from **Rooks Hill Farm** crosses overhead on an impressive, brick arched bridge. Then, 300yds (274m) beyond a **Downs Link** marker post, you'll come to a large Wey South information board on your left hand side. There's some interesting canal history here, and just behind the board lie the muddy remains of the canal itself.

Two brick arches further on, the **Run Common** road crosses overhead. Just beyond the bridge, a 200yds (183m) diversion along the waymarked **Wey South Path** will bring you to **Run Common** itself. You can explore the canal towpath here if you wish, though frankly there's not very much to see.

Now the railway runs straight, climbing imperceptibly onto an embankment. After 750yds (686m), look out for a low brick wall on the left of the track, as the old canal crosses the line at an oblique angle. A little further on, the canal emerges beyond a matching brick wall on your right hand side.

Continue across the railed bridge over **Cranleigh Water**, and through the next brick arch, which carries the B2130 overhead and heralds the outskirts of Cranleigh. New houses sidle up to the line on your left, followed by a small industrial estate and a fork in the track. Turn left here, straight into the car park where your walk began.

WHILE YOU'RE THERE ⓘ

Loseley Park, between Guildford and Godalming, is well worth a visit. The house was built in 1562 by Sir William More, and his descendants still live here. Much of the stone for this lovely Elizabethan building was quarried from the ruins of Waverley Abbey (► Walk 48), and the house also contains panelling from Henry VIII's palace at Nonsuch. You can wander in the magnificent walled gardens, or enjoy a stroll around the nature trail in the park before rounding things off in the tea room and gift shop.

Walk 36

Alfold and the Lost Canal

Take a walk through the wildwoods along a derelict canal tow path.

•DISTANCE•	4¾ miles (7.7km)
•MINIMUM TIME•	2hrs
•ASCENT / GRADIENT•	164ft (50m) ▲ ▲ ▲
•LEVEL OF DIFFICULTY•	🚶 🚶 🚶
•PATHS•	Old canal tow path, field and forest paths. muddy after rain
•LANDSCAPE•	Mainly wooded countryside, some views across farmland
•SUGGESTED MAP•	aqua3 OS Explorer 134 Crawley & Horsham
•START / FINISH•	Grid reference: TQ 026350
•DOG FRIENDLINESS•	On lead in Sidney Wood and Oakhurst Farm
•PARKING•	Forestry Commission car park between Alfold and Dunsfold
•PUBLIC TOILETS•	None on route

BACKGROUND TO THE WALK

As you amble through the depths of Sidney Wood along the sinuous tow path of the long abandoned Wey and Arun canal, you can hardly fail to ponder the significance of this overgrown, muddy trench. In the closing years of the 18th century the Industrial Revolution was in full swing. The roads, such as they were, could simply not cope with carrying coal, heavy raw materials and finished goods over long distances. But in southern England, there was an even more urgent imperative. France was in turmoil and the dawn of a new century found Britain engaged in the Napoleonic Wars. Coastal cargoes in the English Channel were at risk and a new route was needed between London and the South Coast.

Building the Link

River traffic had flowed between London and Guildford since 1653, and the River Arun had been navigable to Pallingham Quay, near Pulborough, since Elizabethan times. All that was needed was a link – and it came in two parts. In 1787, the Arun Navigation was completed northwards from Pallingham Quay to Newbridge Wharf, near Billingshurst. Then, in 1813, Parliament authorised the Wey and Arun Junction Canal between Newbridge and Guildford. It opened in 1816 completing the link between London and the South Coast.

The price of coal in Guildford fell at once by more than 20 per cent, and the canal also carried chalk, timber and agricultural cargoes, reaching a peak of 23,000 tons in 1839. But the railways were already coming and the following year, the London and Southampton forged a new link to the South Coast. There was little immediate impact but in 1865 the London Brighton & South Coast Railway opened between Guildford and Horsham, in direct competition with the canal. Within a few years the waterway was out of business and it was formally abandoned in 1871, though the Arun Navigation struggled on until 1896.

The canal lay derelict for almost a century until, in 1970, enthusiasts established the Wey and Arun Canal Trust. Their aim was to restore navigation between London and the South Coast by reopening the waterway from Guildford to Pallingham Quay. As you'll see on your walk, they still have a mountain to climb. Long stretches remain derelict, and many bridges have been demolished. But 20 bridges and seven locks have already been rebuilt, and over a quarter of the canal's original length will soon be fully restored.

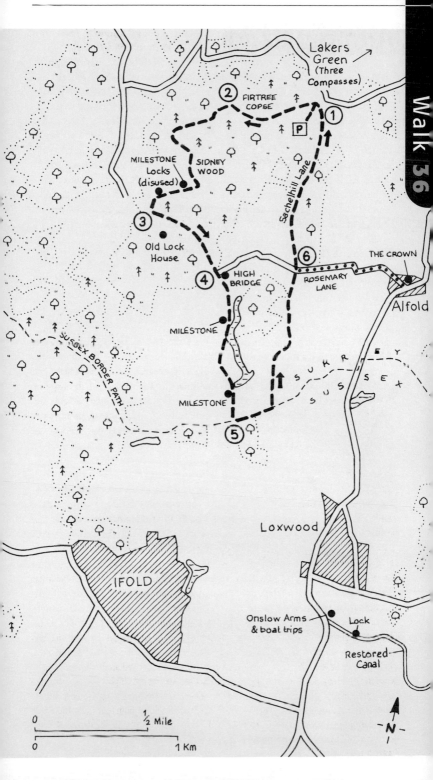

Walk 36

Walk 36

Walk 36 Directions

① From the car park, walk back towards the road for 35yds (32m) until you see a track on your left, marked by a concrete post with a small **Wey South Path** waymark near the top. Turn left, then keep right at the fork 300yds (274m) further on. Cross the tarmac drive at a public bridleway signpost and follow the waymarked path around the edge of **Fir Tree Copse**.

② The **Wey South Path** meets the canal at a gate. Turn left, and follow the tow path for 1 mile (1.6km). Notice the gentle slope as you pass the **Arun 13/Wey 10 milestone**, deep in **Sidney Wood**; it's the only clue that this overgrown section was once the site of a six lock flight.

WHAT TO LOOK FOR ⓘ
The act establishing the Wey and Arun Junction Canal insisted that **milestones** must be installed every half mile along the route so that tolls could be levied accurately. All the original milestones have disappeared, but the Canal Trust is installing new ones at the original locations with a sponsorship scheme raising funds for the restoration project. You'll pass four milestones between Firfield Rough and the Sussex border.

③ A gravelled track crosses the canal at **Sydney Court**. Leave the tow path here and turn left, following the waymarked route across a bridleway crossroads to **High Bridge**.

④ Zig-zag right and left across **Rosemary Lane**, and rejoin the old tow path. After ½ mile (800m) look out for the **Arun 11½/Wey 11½ milestone**, and continue for 150yds (137m) until the **Sussex Border Path** crosses the canal.

⑤ Turn left, and follow the **Sussex Border Path** for 350yds (320m) until the track bends sharply right. Turn left through the metal field gate, and follow the hedge on your right. A second gate leads you past a little cottage; now, follow the public bridleway signpost that points your way through two fields, and through another gate onto a path leading out to **Rosemary Lane**. If you fancy a break, you can turn right here, for the ½ mile (800m) diversion to the **Crown** at **Alfold**.

WHERE TO EAT AND DRINK ⓘ
Head for the **Crown** at Alfold for a friendly, no frills local, although they don't serve food on Sunday or Monday evenings. The canal-side **Onslow Arms** at Loxwood is open all day at weekends, serving traditional pub food and pizzas.

⑥ Otherwise, cross the lane and follow the waymarked bridleway for ½ mile (800m). Now turn left at the public footpath signpost; then, just a few paces past the prominent 'Riding by permit only' sign, turn right up the waymarked footpath through the woods. Fork right a short way further on, then continue over two stiles and follow the path just inside the woodland edge until it bears left and meets the **Wey South Path** at a waymark post. Turn left, and follow the path to the **Sidney Wood** car park road, before turning left again for the short distance back to your car.

WHILE YOU'RE THERE ⓘ
Behind the Onslow Arms at Loxwood you'll find a restored section of the canal where you can travel on board the *Zachariah Keppel*, a 50ft (15m) narrow boat named after the contractor who built the canal. The **Wey and Arun Canal Trust** operates hourly trips on Sunday afternoons between April and October.

Compton's Michelangelo

The charming countryside bordering Loseley Park has some surprises in store.

•DISTANCE•	3¾ miles (6km)
•MINIMUM TIME•	1hr 30min
•ASCENT / GRADIENT•	262ft (80m)
•LEVEL OF DIFFICULTY•	
•PATHS•	Sandy tracks and field paths, can be muddy
•LANDSCAPE•	Farmed and wooded countryside
•SUGGESTED MAP•	aqua3 OS Explorer 145 Guildford & Farnham
•START / FINISH•	Grid reference: SU 963470
•DOG FRIENDLINESS•	On lead through Coneycroft Farm and near livestock. Not allowed in Watts Gallery
•PARKING•	Lay-by in Polsted Lane, close to junction with Withies Lane
•PUBLIC TOILETS•	None on route

BACKGROUND TO THE WALK

During the early 1880s, residents around London's Holland Park might have spotted one of their neighbours hauling an immense statue into his garden on a short length of railway track. The artist and sculptor George Frederic Watts began work on *Physical Energy*, possibly his greatest masterpiece, whilst living at his house in Melbury Road.

Watts created this larger-than-life statue of a horse and rider purely for himself. He'd already worked out the idea as a plaster miniature and he built the full size version in a mixture of chalk, fibre and glue, supported on a wooden framework. You can see both models at the Watts Gallery in Compton, though the finished bronze statue is now in Kensington Gardens, London.

Youthful Talent

Born in 1817, Watts was a sickly child and was educated at home. He studied briefly at the Royal Academy, but dropped out after only a few weeks because he thought that the teaching was 'unfit'. Despite this, he mastered the wide range of styles and techniques that you'll see at the gallery; social paintings, landscapes, allegorical works and sculptures. But, although Watts has been described as the finest portrait painter of his generation, his own gallery has remarkably few of them.

For more than half a century Watts gathered his best works into a 'Hall of Fame' that included artists, authors, scientists and people in public life. He had little interest in money, and saw this collection as his gift to the nation; a public record of the great and the good at a time when photography was still regarded as a passing fashion. As a result, the majority of these paintings are now in the National Portrait Gallery.

Love and Marriage

In his personal life, too, Watts was a difficult person to classify. He married the charismatic actress Ellen Terry in 1864, when he was 47 and his bride was just 17; the consequences were predictable, and the couple separated after only a year. It was more than 20 years before Watts re-married. His new bride, Mary Fraser-Tytler, was a year younger than Ellen, though by now the enormous age difference was rather less significant. In 1891 George and Mary Watts moved to Limnerslease, a new house at Compton designed for them by the architect Ernest George. Here, Mary produced the spectacular Mediterranean-style mortuary chapel (► What To Look For), and the couple commissioned the Watts Gallery, the lovely Arts and Crafts building which opened just a few months before George's death in July, 1904. Limnerslease is now split into three private houses, but you can see the exterior from the back drive to the gallery.

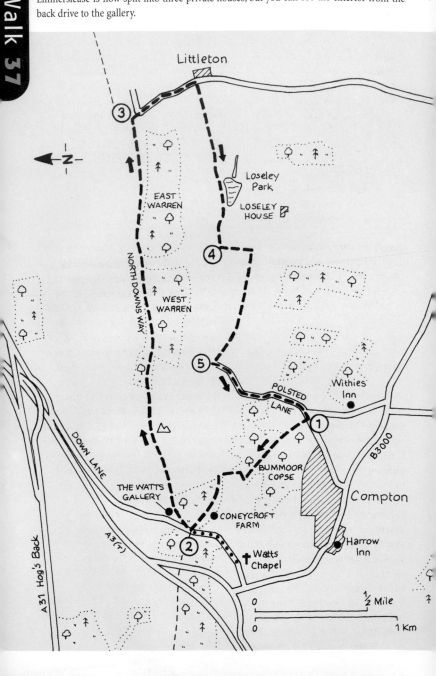

Walk 37 Directions

① Take the signposted public footpath from the lay-by, a few paces from the junction of **Withies Lane** and **Polsted Lane.** Head through **Bummoor Copse**, and leave the woods at a stile. Now follow the woodland edge, zig-zagging right and left over another stile until you clear the woods altogether and come to a waymarked stile at the end of a concrete road. Nip across, and turn left; then, just as you come to the large buildings at **Coneycroft Farm**, dodge up to your right and over a waymarked stile. Follow the narrow path over another stile, and out onto **Down Lane.**

WHAT TO LOOK FOR ⓘ

Take a short diversion along Down Lane, to the **Watts mortuary chapel** in the graveyard at Compton. It was designed by George Watts' wife Mary, who was an artist in her own right. The little terracotta building is shaped like a Celtic cross. George and Mary's grave, with its moulded terracotta kerbstones, lies close to the cloister at the top of the hill.

---

② Turn right for a few paces along the road. Just before the **Watts Gallery**, turn right again onto the signposted **North Downs Way National Trail**; this is fast, easy walking, on a good track with sand under your feet. The track narrows as you pass a few farm buildings and begin the climb towards **West Warren**. Stay with the North Downs Way across a bridleway and into the woods. As you approach **East Warren**, the National Trail zig-zags left and right, and joins a farm road. Follow it for another 700yds (640m) until the outskirts of **Guildford** heave into view and the trail swings left at a waymark post.

③ Turn right here; then, after 50yds (46m) fork right onto **Littleton Lane**. Follow it to the public telephone near **Littleton Youth House**, and turn right onto the signposted public footpath. The path leads you through a succession of open fields, separated by stiles. There's a lake in the fourth field and, beyond the next stile, you'll get some great views of **Loseley House** on your left.

WHERE TO EAT AND DRINK ⓘ

You'll see the **Harrow Inn** on the main road as you drop down from the Hog's Back or the A3. There are main meals in the bar, but you can also get a snack or a sandwich. It's closed on Sunday evenings. The **Withies Inn** is tucked away on Withies Lane. This 16th-century whitewashed free house serves bar snacks and a full restaurant menu.

---

④ Cross the track to **Loseley House** at a stile and four-way signpost, and follow the field edge round to the left. Then, after 50yds (46m), look out for a stile and yellow waymark on your left. Nip across here, and continue in the same direction, but now with the fence on your right. There's a three-way signpost at the next stile; nip across, turn right, and follow the track down a tree-lined avenue all the way through to **Little Polsted** at the top of **Polsted Lane**.

⑤ Turn left, and follow the lane back to the junction where you started your walk.

WHILE YOU'RE THERE ⓘ

Visit the **Watts Gallery**, an engaging exhibition of George Watts' work, from tiny sketchbooks to towering statues. The museum is open on afternoons throughout the year, but closed on Thursdays. Admission is free, though donations towards the museum's upkeep are appreciated.

Trust on Hydon Heath

A circular walk through the varied countryside south of Godalming.

•DISTANCE•	3¾ miles (6km)
•MINIMUM TIME•	1hr 30min
•ASCENT / GRADIENT•	344ft (105m) ▲ ▲ ▲
•LEVEL OF DIFFICULTY•	👫 👫 👫
•PATHS•	Woodland paths, farm tracks and some minor roads
•LANDSCAPE•	Wooded slopes and farmland of Wealden greensand ridge
•SUGGESTED MAP•	aqua3 OS Explorers 133 Haslemere & Petersfield, 145 Guildford & Farnham
•START / FINISH•	Grid reference: SU 979402
•DOG FRIENDLINESS•	On lead through farmyards, near livestock and along roads
•PARKING•	National Trust car park on Salt Lane, near Hydestile
•PUBLIC TOILETS•	None on route

BACKGROUND TO THE WALK

Imagine an organisation so big that its magazine has more readers than The Times, Telegraph and Independent put together. Imagine a landowner whose properties cover an area 30 per cent bigger than the county of Surrey. And imagine a club so popular that its membership outstrips the population of Greater Manchester. That is the measure of the National Trust today. But could you imagine that this vast institution was founded by just three people, one a spinster who died several years before women even had the right to vote?

Bench Mark

At the top of Hydon's Ball, close to the start of this walk, you'll come to a massive granite bench in memory of that very lady. Octavia Hill was a social reformer in the same league as her contemporary, Florence Nightingale. Born in Cambridgeshire in 1838, her father was bankrupted a few years later and her family split up. Octavia and her mother moved to north London, where they began philanthropic work with the Christian Socialists. Octavia witnessed the appalling realities of life in the Dickensian backstreets, and these early experiences inspired the great vocations of her later life; housing reform, and countryside access. During this time, Octavia met her lifelong friend, John Ruskin. He helped launch the first of her many housing improvement schemes and suggested ways of raising capital.

Besides working to improve the conditions in London's slums, Octavia Hill wanted to protect areas of countryside where working people could enjoy their leisure time. She was appalled to see so many green fields disappearing under Victorian suburbs, and she joined the Commons Preservation Society to help safeguard 'open-air sitting rooms for the poor'. Later, she became friends with the society's solicitor, Sir Robert Hunter.

Towards the end of the century, Octavia and Sir Robert joined Canon Rawnsley in his fight for a threatened Lake District beauty spot. This was the campaign that brought together the founding triumvirate of the National Trust; they launched the idea in 1894, and the new organisation was incorporated the following year. Octavia Hill went on to lead many successful appeals and served on the Trust's Council. Soon after her death in 1912, the Trust bought 92 acres (37ha) at Hydon's Ball as her permanent memorial.

Walk 38

THE MERRY
HARRIERS
⑤
HAMBLEDON ROAD
Hambledon
St Peter's
Church
ROBERTSON
OBELISK
PUMPING
STATION ② HYDON HEATH
④ MAPLE Hydon's P ①
BUNGALOW Ball △ ①
179
GREENSAND WAY
UPPER VANN LANE ③
BURGATE
HANGAR
LITTLE
BURGATE FARM
Ⓐ -N-
Ⓓ
½ Mile
SPRING
COPSE ½ Km
THE
HURTWOOD Winkworth
Arboretum
Ⓒ
MARKWICK
FARM
MARKWICK LANE
Hascombe
HASCOMBE
GRANGE
GODALMING
ROAD P Ⓑ WHITE
HORSE

Salt Lane

Walk 38 Directions

① Turn left along the straight forest track a few paces behind the National Trust notice board in the car park. At the crest of the hill, turn right at the eight rustic wooden posts and continue climbing for 180yds (165m) to Octavia Hill's **memorial bench**. Continue straight ahead, leaving the bench on your left. Fork right between three large green inspection covers that give access to the underground reservoirs on the summit of the hill, and drop down the narrow path to a chain link fence on the edge of the National Trust estate.

> **WHILE YOU'RE THERE** ⓘ
> You'll find some dazzling displays of spring and autumn colours just up the road at **Winkworth Arboretum**. This wooded hillside with its two ornamental lakes was laid out during the late 1930s by Dr Wilfrid Fox, and is now cared for by the National Trust. The arboretum includes over 1,000 species of exotic shrubs and trees, including maples, cherries, azaleas and magnolias. As well as exploring the woods themselves, allow time to enjoy the contrasting seasonal views in the area around the lakes.

② Turn left here. After 60yds (55m) you'll see the **Robertson obelisk** on your right. Just beyond this lonely memorial, a maze of little paths will try to lead you astray. Keep as right as you can here, and descend the rutted path to the forest crossroads close to a small water pumping station. Turn left; then, after 200yds (183m), fork right and continue to the parting of the ways 180m (165m) further on. Turn right here, and climb the old sunken way as far as the public bridleway marker post at the top.

③ Turn right here onto the aptly named **Greensand Way**, and continue to **Maple Bungalow**.

④ Pass **Maple Bungalow**, and follow the **Greensand Way** through the valley to **St Peter's Church**, Hambledon. 55yds (50m) beyond the church, fork right at **Court Farm Cottage** and follow the public footpath as it swings, first right, then left, and drops down through a sunken lane to the **Hambledon Road** opposite the **Merry Harriers**.

> **WHERE TO EAT AND DRINK** ⓘ
> The **Merry Harriers** keeps real ales and a cask-conditioned cider, and you can eat for under £5. You'll pass this whitewashed stone and tile hung free house on the Hambledon Road.

⑤ Turn right, along the **Hambledon Road**. Pass **Feathercombe Lane** then, after 200yds (183m), turn right onto a bridleway between open fields back towards **Hydon Heath**. The track enters the woods, and you climb steeply beside the deer fencing on your right. Keep straight on at the end of the fencing and, after 100yds (91m), take the middle track at the three-way junction for the last 350yds (320m) to the car park.

> **WHAT TO LOOK FOR** ⓘ
> As you drop down from the summit of Hydon's Ball, take a moment to pay your respects to the Robertson family. Just off the path, a **small obelisk** records how WA Robertson left the money for the National Trust to buy this area in memory of his two brothers, who were killed in the Great War. Second Lieutenant Laurance Robertson was killed in action during the Battle of the Somme in July 1916, and his brother, Captain Norman Robertson lost his life at Hanover in June the following year.

A Hascombe Loop

Good walking, good views and a good country pub make this a worthwhile extension from Hydon's Ball.
See map and information panel for Walk 38

•DISTANCE•	6¾ miles (11km)
•MINIMUM TIME•	2hr 30min
•ASCENT / GRADIENT•	672ft (205m) ▲▲▲
•LEVEL OF DIFFICULTY•	恭 恭 恭

Walk 39 Directions (Walk 38 option)

Leave the main route at Point ③ and turn left onto the **Greensand Way**, which will carry you all the way through to **Hascombe**. Continue until the track emerges onto **Markwick Lane** at **Little Burgate Farm**. Turn right; then, as the lane levels out, turn left into the woods opposite a public bridleway signpost (Point ④).

Follow the waymarked route as it climbs through a short sunken way, then zig-zag left and right across another path. In the middle of the **Hurtwood**, you'll cross a bridleway; 175yds (160m) further on, fork left. At the next junction, the **Greensand Way** zig zags right, then hard left, and drops steeply down to the White Horse pub in **Hascombe** village (Point ⑤).

Turn right, and follow the **Godalming Road** past the **Old Rectory** and **Hascombe Grange**. On the brow of the hill, opposite **Long Vere House**, nip over the stile on your right and follow the waymarked route as it climbs beside a wooden fence towards the woods.

Bear left, and contour around the edge of the woods until the path swings left down the hill towards **Markwick Lane**. Turn right here, just outside the woodland, and continue to a waymark post where you turn left and drop down to the red clay roofs of **Markwick Farm** (Point ©).

Turn right onto **Markwick Lane**, pass **Handon Cottage** and **Spring Copse**, and climb the hill to a bridleway signpost just over ½ mile (800m) further on (Point ⑩).

Slip away to the left here, ignore the public footpath turning on your left, and contour around the edge of **Burgate Hangar** until the bridleway merges with **Upper Vann Lane** on your left. Follow the lane up the hill, and rejoin the main route at Point ④.

WHAT TO LOOK FOR ⓘ

St Peter's Church at Hascombe rewards closer inspection. By 1863 it had become so dilapidated that the parish commissioned Henry Woodyer to design a completely new one. His little Bargate stone building is a stunning example of Victorian architecture and, inside, you can still see the wonderful painted walls and woodwork which John Betjeman described as 'a Tractarian work of art'.

Walk 40

On the Wey to Godalming

A delightful riverside walk brings you to the charming little town of Godalming.

•DISTANCE•	5 miles (8km)
•MINIMUM TIME•	2hrs
•ASCENT / GRADIENT•	Negligible
•LEVEL OF DIFFICULTY•	
•PATHS•	Riverside tow path, muddy and uneven in a few places
•LANDSCAPE•	Wooded river valley
•SUGGESTED MAP•	aqua3 OS Explorer 145 Guildford & Farnham
•START / FINISH•	Grid reference: SU 991496
•DOG FRIENDLINESS•	Grid reference: SU 966439
•PARKING•	Car park at Godalming Station at end of walk
•PUBLIC TOILETS•	At both railway stations, start and finish
•NOTE•	Park at Godalming and catch train to Guildford

Walk 40 Directions

Leave your car at the end of the walk in Godalming, and catch the train to **Guildford**.

You'll be walking back along the Godalming Navigation, which opened the River Wey to barge traffic between Guildford and Godalming in 1763. 'Navigations' were hybrid waterways – existing rivers tamed by locks and lengths of artificial canal. Barges from London had first reached Guildford over a century earlier, and business was boosted still further when the Basingstoke Canal opened in 1796, followed by the Wey & Arun Canal twenty years later. But commercial traffic on the Wey and Godalming navigations outlasted both of them, and the last barge was unloaded at Coxes Mill, Weybridge, as recently as 1968.

Leave **Guildford Station** by the main entrance and follow the pedestrian signs towards the '**Town Centre via Riverside Walk**'. Turn right when you reach the river, and follow it to the **White House** pub. Continue along Millmead, and rejoin the riverside walk near the *Alice in Wonderland* sculptures just beyond the pub. Pass the **Yvonne Arnaud theatre** on the opposite bank, turn left over the lattice girder bridge opposite Scruffy Murphy's, then turn right at **Millmead Lock**.

WHAT TO LOOK FOR　ⓘ

Go quietly along the more isolated stretches of tow path, and you're more than likely to spot a **grey heron** standing statuesque at the water's edge or rising at your approach and flapping lazily down the river on its huge, powerful wings. Herons are the largest common land birds in the British Isles, and they're impressive by any standards. An adult bird will eat well over a pound of fish every day, making them unpopular with both anglers and fish farmers alike. These wonderful birds have been persecuted since the Middle Ages, and there are still a disturbing number of applications for licences to shoot them.

Pass **Guildford Boat House** with its colourful cluster of narrow boats, then cut across the park and rejoin the tow path at the weir on the far side.

From here the river pushes out into the country. Just before you reach the **Old Ferry footbridge**, look out for a charming little spring on your right; then, beyond the bridge, you'll cross a sandy beach and pass a short wooded section before the approach to **St Catherine's Lock**.

Pass the lock, and continue under the massive girders of the railway as it curves away towards Dorking. There was a railway junction here once; 100yds (91m) further on, look to your right, where a short flight of steps leads up to the old embankment. Here you'll find a Second World War pill box, part of the inland GHQ defence line that extended from the Bristol Channel to the Kent coast.

Next comes **Broadford Bridge** and, a little further on, moorings branch off on the far side of the river along the truncated Wey and Arun Canal (▶ Walk 36). Continue through a little gate with open fields to your right until, just after a second gate, you pass the remains of the old

railway to Cranleigh. Most of this line has now been converted to the Downs Link bridleway, described in Walk 35.

Beyond **Unsted Lock** and the little road from **Tiltham's Farm** comes a lovely meandering section, with views to the woods beyond meadows on your left. Near **Broadwater Park**, the **Manor Inn** restaurant pub backs onto the tow path, with its nice riverside garden and children's play area.

Cross the lane to **Unsted Park**, and continue past **Farncombe Boat House** with its tea room on the far bank. Beyond the colourful moorings at **Catteshall Lock**, industrial buildings intrude briefly into the riverside scene. Now the river bends hard right at **Godalming Wharf**, and in no time you arrive at the Town Bridge next to Godalming United Church.

Turn left over the bridge, continue straight up **Bridge Street** past Waitrose, and bear right into **High Street** at the top of the hill. Carry on to the **Pepperpot** – the unlikely name of the 1814 Market Hall – and fork right down **Church Street**. Pass the **Church of St Peter and St Paul** on your right, bear left into Station Road, then turn right into Station Approach and the car park where your walk began.

Pirbright, I Presume

A flexible figure-of-eight walk, starting from Pirbright's vast village green.

•DISTANCE•	4¾ miles (7.7km)
•MINIMUM TIME•	2hrs
•ASCENT / GRADIENT•	114ft (35m) ▲ ▲ ▲
•LEVEL OF DIFFICULTY•	👫 👫 👫
•PATHS•	Country roads, woodland tracks and paths, boggy in places, patchy waymarking
•LANDSCAPE•	Wooded farmland conceals several massive houses on edge of Pirbright army ranges
•SUGGESTED MAP•	aqua3 OS Explorer 145 Guildford & Farnham
•START / FINISH•	Grid reference: SU 946560
•DOG FRIENDLINESS•	On lead on road and in woods south of Admiral's Walk
•PARKING•	On village green in Pirbright
•PUBLIC TOILETS•	None on route

BACKGROUND TO THE WALK

Whether or not Stanley actually delivered the famous one-liner 'Dr Livingstone, I presume?', when he tracked down the ailing missionary-explorer at Ujiji on Lake Tanganyika, the expression has passed into legend. So you can be forgiven for experiencing a profound sense of disbelief when your own expedition into deepest Surrey uncovers Stanley's grave in a quiet corner of a village churchyard. You might expect to find it in Highgate Cemetery, perhaps; or, as Stanley himself had wished, next to the great Dr Livingstone in Westminster Abbey. But St Michael and All Angels, Pirbright? Well, sometimes fact can be stranger than fiction and, a few minutes into your walk, you'll come face to face with Stanley's powerfully simple memorial.

The Background Story

But we've run a bit ahead of the walk and the story here, so it's worth going back to the beginning. In January 1841, Elisabeth Parry gave birth to an illegitimate child at Denbigh, in North Wales. The boy was baptised after his father – John Rowlands – who died just a couple of years later. Young John spent most of his childhood in the poverty-stricken surroundings of St Asaph's workhouse, until he ran away to sea and worked a passage to New Orleans in the USA. There, he took the name of his adoptive father, an American merchant called Henry Morton Stanley.

A Passion for Africa

With his new identity, Stanley served in the Confederate army during the American civil war and went on to become a special correspondent for the New York Herald. At that time David Livingstone, who was in Africa searching for the source of the River Nile, had been out of touch for some five years. Most people believed that he was dead but, in 1869, Stanley accepted his editor's commission to find him.

It was March 1871 before Stanley led a company of around 2,000 men from Zanzibar into the uncharted African interior. Inevitably, there were problems; people deserted, disease was rife, and there were tribal conflicts along the way. Nevertheless, 700 miles (1,134km) and 236 days later, Stanley finally caught up with the ailing Livingstone and nursed him back to health. The two men went on to explore the northern end of Lake Tanganyika together before Stanley returned to Europe in 1872.

Stanley's subsequent expeditions opened up the centre of the continent, and led to the foundation of the Belgian dominated Congo Free State (which later became Zaire and is now called the Democratic Republic of Congo). His career in Africa ended with a successful three year mission to rescue Mehmed Emin Pasha, a German explorer and provincial governor, pinned down by a native uprising. In the closing years of the 19th century Stanley returned to England, married, and moved to Furze Hill, near Pirbright. He spent five years as the Liberal Unionist MP for North Lambeth, and was knighted in 1899. He died in May, 1904.

Walk 41

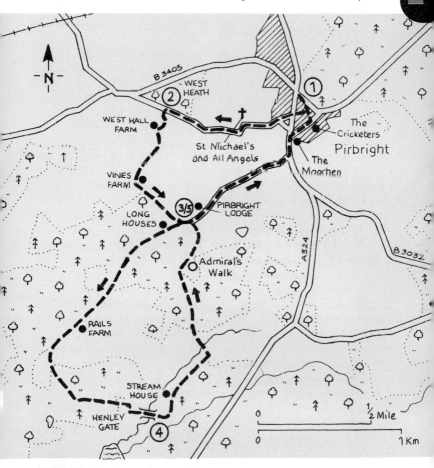

Walk 41 Directions

① Turn right out of the car park, and bear right across **the green**. Cross the main road, follow the lane towards the church, and turn into the churchyard at the little gate on your right. Just inside, you'll see Stanley's massive, roughly-hewn memorial, bearing his African name 'Bula Matari' and the single word 'AFRICA'. His wife, Dorothy, lies in the same little plot, edged with miniature standing stones and neatly clipped yew hedging. Don't miss the lovely interior of this beautifully kept Georgian church - and look, too, for Stanley's other memorial, an inlaid brass plaque on the wall opposite the entrance.

WHILE YOU'RE THERE ⓘ

Only the finest malt, hops, yeast and water find their way into the range of traditional cask conditioned and bottled beers produced at the **Hog's Back Brewery**. The brewery shop and free viewing gallery are open seven days a week; you'll see the brewers at work on any weekday, and there are beer tastings too. The brewery is based in converted 18th-century barns at Manor Farm, Tongham, just off the Hog's Back on the outskirts of Farnham.

Leave the churchyard by the lychgate, and turn right along the lane. Pass the **Old School House** and **West Heath**, and continue for 200yds (183m).

② Turn left down the signposted bridleway towards **West Hall Farm**. Follow the track as it winds through the farmyard and joins a gated green lane. Continue past **Vines Farm** to the edge of a small birchwood and turn left along the muddy woodland track. Bear right just beyond the power lines and continue to the junction of tracks near a letter box in the wall at **Pirbright Lodge.**

WHERE TO EAT AND DRINK ⓘ

Choose from two pubs on Pirbright's village green. Locals head for the **Cricketers**, where there's a good range of snacks and bar meals, plus daily specials. A few doors away, the **Moorhen** follows the Vintage Inns formula with its flagstone floors, beamed ceilings and roaring log fires in winter. You'll find something to eat here all day, every day.

WHAT TO LOOK FOR ⓘ

In the woods between Stream House and Admiral's Walk, you'll walk between clumps of **rhododendron bushes** with their sprawling branches and dark, evergreen leaves. Introduced from the Himalayas to provide cover for pheasants on sporting estates, these huge shrubs thrive on acid soils. They're much admired for their displays of springtime colour, but foresters have little love for the species; they can run out of control, choking the native woodland flora.

---

③ Double back hard right, and follow the broad track past **Long Houses**. Keep left at the fork, and pass **Rails Farm** and **Kiln Cottage**, where the track narrows briefly before bearing left onto the Pirbright ranges perimeter track. As you approach the military barrier at **Henley Gate**, bear left onto a broad woodland track and follow it through to a T-junction. Turn right; then, 40yds (37m) further on, turn left onto a waymarked bridleway and continue until you cross a small stream.

④ Turn left onto a signposted bridleway, pass **Stream House**, then follow the green lane just to the right of **Bourne House**. Continue for 300yds (274m), until a waymark post points your way into the woods on your left. Continue over a stile and up the side of a small field, then cross the plank bridge into a boggy area of rough woodland. Keep straight on until you reach the second waymark post, then bear right onto a forest road and follow it back to **Pirbright Lodge.**

⑤ Turn right, and follow the lane out to the A324. Cross over, and turn left onto the roadside pavement that leads you back to **the green** where your walk began.

The Puttenham Tales

A varied walk in the shadow of the Hog's Back, taking in a section of the North Downs Way.

·DISTANCE·	4 miles (6.4km)
·MINIMUM TIME·	1hr 45min
·ASCENT / GRADIENT·	295ft (90m) ▲▲▲
·LEVEL OF DIFFICULTY·	林 林 林
·PATHS·	Woodland tracks and field edge paths
·LANDSCAPE·	Wooded heath and farmland
·SUGGESTED MAP·	aqua3 OS Explorer 145 Guildford & Farnham
·START / FINISH·	Grid reference: SU 920461
·DOG FRIENDLINESS·	Can run free on Puttenham Common, on lead in village
·PARKING·	Puttenham Common top car park
·PUBLIC TOILETS·	None on route

BACKGROUND TO THE WALK

The railway line no longer runs to Hayfield, high in the Derbyshire Peak District. With it have passed many of the 400 people who gathered at the little station for the mass trespass on Kinder Scout in 1932. But what has that to do with a gentle walk in the Surrey countryside? Have you stumbled into a different book? Not at all. The 1930s saw an explosion of interest in walking, and the Kinder Scout trespass was a landmark along the way to the legislation which underpins the modern family of National Trails. First was the Pennine Way, opened in 1965; but other routes soon followed.

The Pilgrim's Way

In September 1978 the North Downs Way was officially opened between Farnham and Dover, and you'll follow a section of it on your way through Puttenham today. In many places, the route follows the old Pilgrim's Way that runs from Winchester, through Farnham and Guildford to Canterbury. The National Trail has a loop that allows modern-day pilgrims to visit Canterbury on their way to or from Dover, but you don't need to walk all the way to Becket's cathedral to enjoy a few stories of the road.

Tales From the Trail

About 400yds (366m) before you reach the North Downs Way, near the entrance to a Woodland Trust property on your right, you'll pass a bridleway which was part of the old carriage drive to Hampton Park. Legend has it that when Richard Brinsley Sheridan was visiting his friend Edward Long at Hampton in the early years of the nineteenth century, his coach turned over at this spot. Long subsequently planted seven trees to mark the route; one for each of his daughters.

A little further on, where a line of trees marks the path from Lascombe Farm out onto the common, you'll see the remains of an old wooden gate. This is Highfield Hatch, one of the 'hatches' or gates that were placed around the common to prevent grazing animals from straying onto the arable fields. General James Oglethorpe, who founded the American state of Georgia, bought the Puttenham estate in 1744. However, he actually lived in Godalming, and he sold the estate in 1761. The new owner demolished the little manor house, and built the Palladian mansion that you'll see from the footpath off Suffield Lane, just after leaving the North Downs Way. Although he renamed it 'The Priory', the building never had any religious connections.

As you say goodbye to the North Downs Way, cast your mind back to Hayfield and its little railway – because, appropriately enough, the old trackbed has now been turned into a very pleasant footpath.

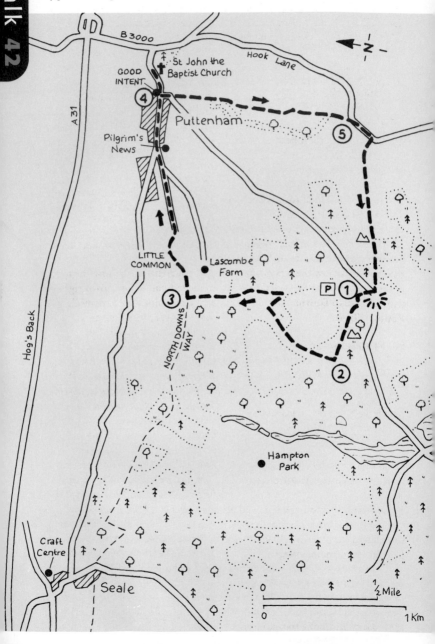

Walk Walk **42 Directions**

① Head into the view from the car park, dropping down into the trees with a wooden handrail on your right. Fork left through the woods, and bear right when the path forks again 100yd (91m) further on. After 150yds (137m) you'll cross another track at a tiny clearing.

② Turn right here and pass a green and mauve banded waymark post. Keep straight on until you reach two similar posts 300yds (274m) further on. Fork right here, onto a narrow path that climbs gently through the bracken. Continue for 25yds (23m) beyond a line of electricity wires, then turn right, onto a broad sandy track. After 150yds (137m), turn sharp left onto a similar track. Pass a large white house on your right, then, ignoring all turnings, follow the waymarked public bridleway to the junction with the **North Downs Way National Trail**.

WHAT TO LOOK FOR
Visit the **Church of St John the Baptist** in Puttenham. As you enter the churchyard, you'll see a well on the left, last used around 1750 when the church caught fire. It was filled in and forgotten about until 1972, when it was dramatically rediscovered. During morning service on Palm Sunday the first of a line of recently planted yew trees suddenly disappeared down the well.

③ Turn sharp right here and follow the **North Downs Way** as it winds over **Little Common** and continues through **Puttenham** village.

④ Turn right opposite the **Good Intent**, into **Suffield Lane**. As the lane swings to the right, nip over the stile by the public footpath

signpost on your left, and follow the left-hand edge of an open field to the trees on the far side. Now take the waymarked route over a second stile to the left of the woods. Two more stiles now lead you away from the woods, keeping a post and wire fence on your right hand side. Cross the stile beside a prominent oak tree and keep straight ahead, through the metal field gate. Bear right down a short, sharp slope towards the woods, and jump the stile leading out onto **Hook Lane**.

WHILE YOU'RE THERE
The **Manor Farm Craft Centre** is tucked away in picturesque old buildings in the middle of Seale village, just along the road from Puttenham. You can visit the different craftsmen and women in their native habitat, and watch demonstrations of jewellery, calligraphy, knitwear and many others. There's also a craft shop, and a tea room. Closed Mondays.

⑤ Turn right, and follow the road to the left hand bend. Turn right again, over the stile by a public footpath sign. Three more stiles bring you to a 'right of way' waymark; bear right here, and follow the post and wire fence on your right. Continue to a small wood, step over a wooden barrier into an old sunken lane, and keep straight on for 150yds (137m) to a small waymark post. Turn left for just a few paces, then right at a second waymark. Climb steeply here, for the short way back to **Suffield Lane** and the entrance to the car park where you started.

WHERE TO EAT AND DRINK
Puttenham is handily placed, half-way round the walk. **Pilgrim's News** sells snacks and ices to eat on the hoof. For something more substantial, the **Good Intent** at the other end of The Street serves real ales and bar meals.

Through Wild Chobham

An easy-to-follow circuit of Chobham's surprisingly wild and open heathland.

•DISTANCE•	3 miles (4.8km)
•MINIMUM TIME•	1hr
•ASCENT / GRADIENT•	147ft (45m)
•LEVEL OF DIFFICULTY•	
•PATHS•	Broad bridleway tracks, can be boggy in places
•LANDSCAPE•	Rolling heathland with some wooded areas
•SUGGESTED MAP•	aqua3 OS Explorer 160 Windsor, Weybridge & Bracknell
•START / FINISH•	Grid reference: SU 973648
•DOG FRIENDLINESS•	Keep dogs under control, especially near grazing animals
•PARKING•	Staple Hill car park, between Chobham and Longcross
•PUBLIC TOILETS•	Chobham village car park

BACKGROUND TO THE WALK

Consider this. There are only around 60 species of butterflies in the British Isles – and you can see 29 of them on the sweeping expanses of Chobham Common. The litany of flora and fauna goes on; for instance, rather more than 200 species of birds live in this country or visit regularly, and over a hundred of them have been recorded on Chobham's lowland heaths. It all helps to explain why Chobham Common isn't just the largest National Nature Reserve in South East England, it's also one of Europe's best protected wildlife sites.

A Good Address

As any estate agent will tell you, the three most important things to consider when looking for somewhere to live are location, location and location. That's true for wildlife too and, for many species, heathland is the ideal home. But lowland heaths themselves can only survive in certain specific places. They won't develop across most of continental Europe, with its hot summers and harsh winters; they need a more temperate climate, found around the western seaboard and on offshore islands like Britain. The geology is also an important factor, and heaths just love the acid conditions of Surrey's gravels, sands and clays.

With all this going for it, you'd guess that heathland has a pretty secure future. Unfortunately not; this artificial habitat is the product of thousands of years of clearance, cultivation and grazing. As agriculture has intensified, traditional methods have all but died out. Many acres of heathland have reverted to scrub or dense 'secondary' woodland which, unlike the ancient woods, has relatively little wildlife value. So, as at Headley (➤ Walk 21), conservation of the common is mainly about preserving the open heathland vegetation. At Chobham, you're likely to see grazing with traditional breeds of cattle, and you may encounter more modern methods of management; heather cutting, tree clearance and turf stripping, replicating the traditional harvesting of building materials and fuel.

But the real reason for coming to Chobham is to revel in the wide horizons, the fresh air, and the astonishing variety of wildlife. Above the tracts of ling and bell heather you may be lucky enough to see a hobby, the miniature falcon which, at a distance, looks like a huge swift. Closer to the ground, look out for sand lizards and harmless smooth snakes, as well as for orchids and insectivorous sundews. Pack your binoculars, and a decent field guide!

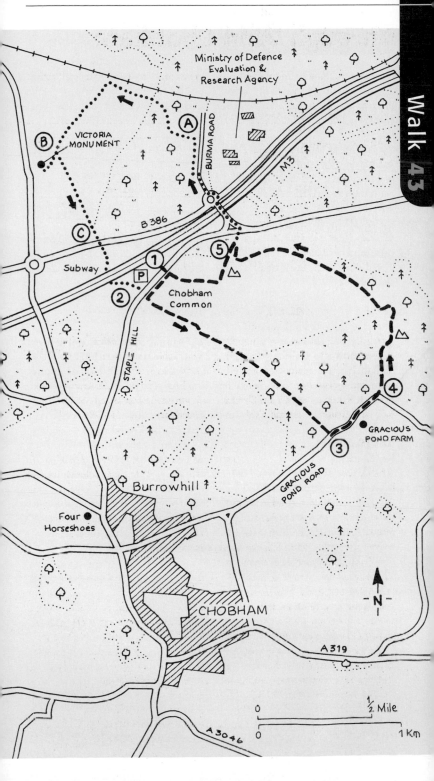

Walk **43**

Walk 43 Directions

① Cross the road from the car park, and turn right onto the sandy track running parallel with the road on your right.

② In little more than 200yds (183m) you'll rejoin the road at a locked barrier; turn hard left here, onto the waymarked horse ride that will carry you straight across the middle of the common. There are several crossroads and turnings, but simply keep walking straight ahead until you reach **Gracious Pond Road**.

③ Turn left onto the road, pass the attractive thatched buildings of **Gracious Pond Farm**, and continue to the sharp right hand bend. Keep straight on here, up the signposted footpath. A few paces further on the track bends to the right; keep straight on again, plunging into the woods at a wooden barrier gate and keeping left at the fork 50yds (46m) further on.

④ Follow the path as it climbs gently through a conifer plantation until, just beyond the power lines, another path merges from your right and you arrive at a waymarker post. Follow the bridleway around to the left, cross a small brook, and fork right at the next waymarker post. Now simply follow the bridleway, ignoring all side turnings, until you come to a waymarker post at a distorted crossroads junction. Bear right here until, a few paces beyond a wooden sleeper causeway on your right, you reach another waymarker post.

> **WHILE YOU'RE THERE** ⓘ
> A short drive from Chobham will bring you to the gentle landscapes of the **Savill Gardens**, on the southern outskirts of Windsor Great Park. Sir Eric Savill created his woodland gardens to show the best of every season, from springtime daffodils and azaleas right through to winter evergreens and the indoor displays in the Queen Elizabeth Temperate House. The gardens are open daily all year, and feature a nice summerhouse-style restaurant.

⑤ Swing hard left here, and follow the track as it bears around to the left before getting into its stride and heading, straight as an arrow, in an obvious line across the open heath. After about 300yds (274m) take the first waymarked footpath on your right, and follow the narrow path up through the gorse and over a wooden sleeper causeway. At the top of the hill, you'll recognise the wooden barrier just a few paces from the road. Cross over the road, back to the **car park** where your walk began.

> **WHAT TO LOOK FOR** ⓘ
> Amongst the many different fungi that emerge on the common in autumn, you're sure to recognise the **fly agaric** (*Amanita muscaria*). The dome-shaped cap is the colour of tomato soup, flecked with little creamy-white scales, and the fungus is so familiar from children's books that you almost expect to see a fairy sitting on top. This poisonous species gets its name from the north European habit of crumbling the cap in milk and using the mixture to kill flies.

> **WHERE TO EAT AND DRINK** ⓘ
> The whitewashed **Four Horseshoes** is set back on the green at Burrowhill and serves a variety of snacks and daily specials. In Chobham, you'll find the **Saddlers Halt Restaurant & Tea Rooms** with its open air courtyard, popular with walkers. The **Sun Inn** offers a good choice of bar meals and snacks.

Chobham on Parade

Cross the M3 motorway for a longer walk exploring the military associations on Chobham's northern heaths.

See map and information panel for Walk 43

•DISTANCE•	5 miles (8km)
•MINIMUM TIME•	2hrs
•ASCENT / GRADIENT•	213ft (65m)
•LEVEL OF DIFFICULTY•	

Walk 44 Directions (Walk 43 option)

Leave the main route at Point ⑤, and keep straight on until you reach a small car park close to the junction of **Staple Hill** and the B386. Cross right over, turn left, and bear right across the M3 motorway. Keep straight on at the roundabout, and follow the **Burma Road** until just after the right hand bend. Turn in to the left here; then, 30yds (27m) further on, turn right at the waymark post. Continue to the next waymarked bridleway crossroads (Point Ⓐ).

Turn left, and continue along the gravelled track as it bears around to the right past another waymark post. Now follow the track as it loops its way through light woodland, where you may catch sight of a train on the railway to your right. The path clears the woodland, bends round to the left, and continues to an oblique bridleway crossroads and waymark post at Point Ⓑ.

You'll need to bear left here; but a short diversion straight ahead will bring you to the lollipop-shaped

Victoria monument, (► What To Look For) just off the path in the bushes, near a bench seat on your right. After visiting the monument, retrace your steps to Point Ⓑ and turn right. Now simply ignore all the side turnings, and follow the well maintained bridleway straight back through the gorse and scrub to the B386 (Point Ⓒ).

WHAT TO LOOK FOR ⓘ

Beyond the brooding presence of the MOD research establishment at Longcross, close to the start of this walk, you'll find a more picturesque reminder of Chobham's military history. In June 1853, as Britain, France, Turkey and Russia were manoeuvering towards war in the Crimea, Queen Victoria reviewed more than 8,000 of her troops on this lonely heathland. Shortly after her death almost half a century later, the parishioners commemorated the event with a simple granite cross 'in memory of the noble life of Queen Victoria'.

Cross straight over, and follow the signposted route as the bridleway burrows under the M3. Fork left just beyond the motorway, and continue as the track winds to the left and brings you to a small car park on the north side of **Staple Hill**. Cross over the road and turn to your left to rejoin the main route at Point ②.

Jessop's Jaunt: the Basingstoke Canal

A peaceful canalside walk through the heart of Surrey's commuter belt.

•DISTANCE•	6 miles (9.7km)
•MINIMUM TIME•	2hrs 30min
•ASCENT / GRADIENT•	Negligible
•LEVEL OF DIFFICULTY•	
•PATHS•	Canal tow path, generally well-maintained, but some occasional muddy patches
•LANDSCAPE•	Gentle, wooded, canalside scenery
•SUGGESTED MAP•	aqua3 OS Explorer 145 Guildford & Farnham
•START•	Grid reference: SU 892533
•FINISH•	Grid reference: SU 951569
•DOG FRIENDLINESS•	Good, but scoop the poop
•PARKING•	Brookwood Station
•PUBLIC TOILETS•	Mytchett Canal Centre
•NOTE•	Park at end of walk and catch train to Ash Vale

Walk 45 Directions

Park at Brookwood Station, and catch the train to **Ash Vale**.

You won't see much of the canal from the train, so this is a good moment to catch up on a little history. The Basingstoke Canal was built late in the 18th century, to carry agricultural cargoes between mid-Hampshire and the capital. After an early proposal for a line northwards to the River Thames at Bray proved too costly, the present route was surveyed by William Jessop and opened in 1794.

Right from the start, traffic was lighter than expected, and grandiose plans for extensions to Southampton and Bristol came to nothing. Trade picked up during the 1830s, carrying construction materials for the London &

Southampton Railway. But the canal was digging its own grave; railway competition simply made things worse and, by 1866, the company was bankrupt. The business soldiered on under a succession of different owners, but the writing was on the wall when Greywell tunnel, six miles east of Basingstoke, collapsed in 1932.

> **WHILE YOU'RE THERE** ⓘ
>
> Not far from the start of your walk is the **Basingstoke Canal Centre** at Mytchett. Besides the small bookshop and tea room, you'll find a surprisingly good exhibition about the canal and its history. There's a replica canal barge cabin, display boards and interactive videos, together with bits and pieces of canal memorabilia. Finally, you'll leave through a spooky mock-up of Greywell Tunnel.

By the mid-1960s the canal had become little more than an overgrown marsh, and the newly-formed Surrey & Hampshire Canal

Society began a campaign for public ownership and restoration as a leisure amenity. It was a winning formula, and in 1991 the canal was re-opened all the way to Greywell. The Greywell Tunnel itself has long been colonised by bats and, despite some restoration on the western side, it now seems unlikely that the canal will return to Basingstoke.

Your train should have arrived in **Ash Vale** by now. Drop down the steps out of the station, and turn left up **Station Approach**. Almost at the end of the road you'll see the canal, down a short concrete ramp on your right. Walk down to the tow path, turn left under the railway bridge, and continue with the canal on your right-hand side.

ⓘ WHERE TO EAT AND DRINK

The **Canal Centre tea room** at Mytchett offers a nice range of home-made teas, snacks and daily specials, as well as traditional Sunday lunches. It's open Tuesday to Sunday between April and September, and weekends only during the winter. At the end of the walk you'll find the **Brookwood Hotel**, next to the station. It's open all day, has imaginative menus and Brookwood Best bitter.

At first, you'll be walking beside the backs of the houses in **Ash Vale**; then the railway draws alongside, and soon you'll see the canal centre at **Mytchett**, just across a little swing bridge. Beyond the canal centre you enter the wooded section running almost unbroken to

Walk 45

Brookwood. You'll pass **Frimley Lodge Park**, where enthusiasts operate a miniature railway on Sundays and Bank Holidays.

The tow path changes sides at the **Guildford Road bridge** which, like several of the bridges along the canal, has been painstakingly reconstructed to the original design. Just beyond the bridge, you'll cross the aqueduct over the main London-to-Southampton railway; it was built in 1838, and extended when the railway was widened in about 1900.

Next comes the high concrete bridge at **Deepcut**, heralding the ½ mile (800m) cutting that gives the area its name. It leads you to **Frimley Lock**, and the start of the sinuous 14-lock flight that leads the canal down to **Brookwood**. This is a lovely section, shaded by young oak trees, and the locks themselves blend into the landscape like ornamental temples in some stately pleasure ground.

Just past the pink cottage at **Pirbright Lock** the tow path changes sides again, and you zig-zag left and right across **Pirbright Bridge**. Continue for a further 850yds (778m), until you reach a green lattice girder bridge. Cross the canal here, signposted towards Brookwood, and walk up **Sheets Heath Lane** to the station where your walk began.

ⓘ WHAT TO LOOK FOR

Just beyond the station subway, **Brookwood cemetery** is something rather unusual – a kind of overspill town for London's dead. In 1851, when cremation was still illegal and the capital's graveyards were reaching capacity, the London Necropolis Company established this cemetery on Woking Common. It had its own branch railway, with stations for the special 'coffin trains' from Waterloo. Since then, huge areas have been dedicated to the 20th-century's war dead; the sheer scale of the place is awesome, and you can still trace part of the old railway's route through the grounds.

Witley's Follies and Frauds

This walk sets out along the Greensand Way, and finishes in the Old Bailey!

•DISTANCE•	6 miles (9.7km)
•MINIMUM TIME•	2hrs 45min
•ASCENT / GRADIENT•	558ft (170m) ▲▲▲
•LEVEL OF DIFFICULTY•	🚶🚶 🚶🚶 🚶🚶
•PATHS•	Woodland tracks and paths across farmland, some short sections on minor roads
•LANDSCAPE•	Pretty landscape of small fields and wooded valleys
•SUGGESTED MAP•	aqua3 OS Explorer 133 Haslemere & Petersfield
•START / FINISH•	Grid reference: SU 907397
•DOG FRIENDLINESS•	By law, dogs must be on lead through Furzefield Wood
•PARKING•	Lay-by on Dyehouse Road, 60yds (55m) west of junction with Old Portsmouth Road near Thursley
•PUBLIC TOILETS•	None on route

BACKGROUND TO THE WALK

As you head east along the edge of Witley Common on your way back towards Thursley, two grey stone lodges stand sentinel at the entrances to Witley Park. Nowadays, an exclusive business and conference centre lies beyond these gateways; but, at the close of the 19th century, the estate was put together by a very different kind of business man.

Whitaker Wright was a financier and self-made millionaire. He had mining interests around the world and, closer to home, his business empire included the London & Globe Finance Company, principal backers of London's Bakerloo line.

Pushing the Boat Out

About 1890 Wright assembled a huge 9,000 acre (3,644ha) estate stretching from Thursley to the Devil's Punchbowl and engaged leading architects and engineers to construct a vast mansion and lavish pleasure gardens. But whatever the scale of the house and grounds, it's Wright's dream-like follies that send your imagination into overdrive.

Like a children's den, it all starts with a hollow tree and a door. Beyond the door, a ramp spirals down past musty subterranean rooms towards a flooded tunnel, 50ft (15m) below the ground. Your feet would take you no further; but luckily enough, there's a boat here. Climb aboard, and feel your way through the tunnel until it brings you out onto a lake.

There's an island over there. Row across and tie up the boat; things are starting to get interesting. A flight of stairs lead down to a light, airy room directly below the island. Time to change into party clothes here, before more steps and another tunnel take you through to the miniature iron and glass ballroom, totally submerged beneath the surface of the lake. If you'd like a dance, only the fish will notice. Another submarine tunnel leads us back into the warm sunshine, to ponder what all this must have cost. It's said that Wright spent around £1.5m on Witley Park in the 1890's; perhaps as much as £200m by today's standards. But that was the least of it.

By the turn of the century, Wright's business enterprises were collapsing like a set of dominoes; he was arrested on charges of fraud, tried at the Old Bailey, and sentenced to seven years imprisonment. Waiting in an anteroom to the court, Whitaker Wright had other ideas. He asked for a cigar, and a glass of whiskey – then swallowed a cyanide capsule, and died where he fell.

Sadly, you cannot see any of Wright's follies. The entire Witley Park estate is private property, and not open to the public at any time. Please keep to the rights of way described. You can find a good description of what lies beyond the estate boundaries in *Follies, Grottoes and Garden Buildings* by Gwyn Headley and Wim Meulenkamp (Aurum Press, 1999).

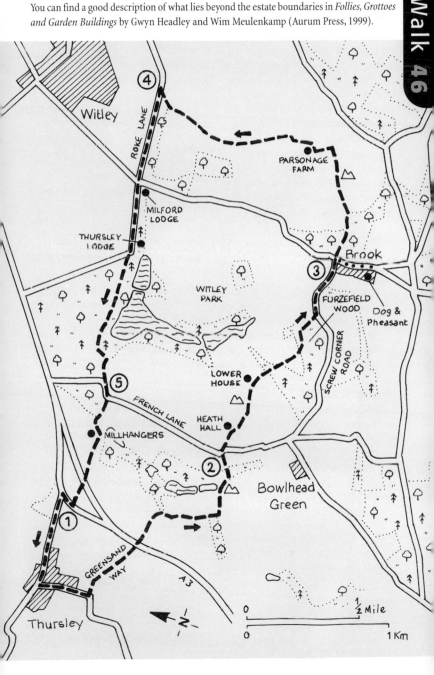

Walk 46

Walk 46 **Directions**

① Follow the pavement towards **Thursley**, pass the village hall, and turn left into **The Street**. When the road bends sharp right, turn left onto the waymarked **Greensand Way**; this signposted bridleway will lead you through a small metal gate and across an open field to the A3. Cross carefully, and follow the waymarked route towards **Cosford Farm**. As the lane drops past **Cosford Farm**, continue along the green lane to the foot of the hill and fork left. The waymarked **Greensand Way** climbs steeply through the woods, crosses two stiles, and leads to **French Lane**.

WHAT TO LOOK FOR

In a field near Heath Hall Farm, you'll pass a typical **old shepherd's hut** made from corrugated iron with glass windows and small iron wheels. Huts like these were towed onto the Downs during the lambing season, so that the shepherd could keep a watch over his flock. A good shepherd was a valued asset, earning around 35/- (£1.75) a week in the late 19th century. Besides his wages, the shepherd would have a free cottage and garden, together with free coal and firewood and an allowance for his dog.

② Cross over, and continue through an avenue of small trees, over a stile, and around the edge of an field. Half-way along the side of the field, dodge left through a wicket gate, cross the drive to **Heath Hall**, and follow the waymarked route to the edge of **Furzefield Wood**. Turn left through the woods, then left onto **Screw Corner Road**.

③ Continue across the A286 and follow the **Greensand Way** until it turns off to the right, near the top of the hill. Keep straight on along the blue waymarked bridleway to **Parsonage Farm Cottages**; turn left here, and follow the footpath as it zig-zags around **Parsonage Farm**. Cross the farm lane, and head for the stile on the far side of the field. Nip over and follow the path through the gently curving valley until two stiles lead you past a pair of white cottages. Bear right up the cottage drive to **Roke Lane**.

WHILE YOU'RE THERE

The **Grayshott Pottery**, near Hindhead, was founded in 1956, but traces its roots from Mary Watts' pottery at the Watts Gallery in Compton (▶ Walk 37). You can watch the potters making a range of stoneware and porcelain, browse in the shop and have a cup of coffee.

④ Turn left, re-cross the A286 at **Milford Lodge**, and continue along **Lea Coach Road** to **Thursley Lodge**. You'll get a glimpse of **Witley Park** down the private drive here, but your route lies along the bridleway straight ahead. The lane drops down to a junction; swing left past **Eastlake** and **Lake Lodge**, then bear right onto a woodland path.

⑤ Turn left briefly onto **French Lane**, then fork right onto the signposted bridleway which winds through Milhanger's landscaped grounds and up to the A3. Cross the road, and continue onto the bridleway directly opposite. Follow it to the **Old Portsmouth Road**; turn right, then left into **Dyehouse Road** and back to the lay-by where your walk began.

WHERE TO EAT AND DRINK

A 5 minute diversion at Brook brings you to the tile-hung **Dog and Pheasant**, swathed under a mass of colourful Virginia creeper. You can get morning coffee here as well as a range of meals.

Murder on the Hindhead Road

A charming, varied circuit at one of Surrey's best known beauty spots.

•DISTANCE•	3½ miles (5.7km)
•MINIMUM TIME•	1hr 30min
•ASCENT / GRADIENT•	394ft (120m) ▲▲▲
•LEVEL OF DIFFICULTY•	🚶 🚶 🚶
•PATHS•	Mostly broad, unmade forest tracks
•LANDSCAPE•	Plunging, dramatic woods and heathland
•SUGGESTED MAP•	aqua3 OS Explorer 133 Haslemere & Petersfield
•START / FINISH•	Grid reference: SU 890357
•DOG FRIENDLINESS•	Take care at A3 crossings, watch for grazing animals
•PARKING•	Hillcrest car park, on A3 just east of Hindhead
•PUBLIC TOILETS•	At car park

BACKGROUND TO THE WALK

How times change! Today, Hindhead Common and the Devil's Punch Bowl are renowned beauty spots, lovingly cared for by the National Trust. Yet, three centuries ago, this desolate area was dreaded by travellers on the Portsmouth road. Daniel Defoe thought it barren and sterile, 'horrid and frightful to look on' and, even after the road was tunpiked and improved in 1749, travellers were not entirely safe.

Companions of the Road

One Sunday in September 1786, an unknown sailor with money in his pocket was making his way towards Portsmouth when he fell into the company of three other travellers; Michael Casey, Edward Lonegon and James Marshall. One of these three was apparently a former shipmate, and the four of them stopped at the Red Lion in Thursley for food and drink. The trio, it seems, were penniless, so their new found friend paid the bill before they all set off over the Devil's Punch Bowl towards Portsmouth.

Probably we shall never know whether the brutal murder on the summit east of Hindhead was anything more than simple robbery. But, whatever the motive, Casey, Lonegon and Marshall set about their companion, stabbing him repeatedly before stripping his body, rolling it down the hill into the Punch Bowl, and scurrying off towards Liphook. The spot is still marked by a memorial stone erected 'in detestation of a barbarious murder committed here on an unknown sailor'; you'll see it on the left of the old road, soon after the start of your walk.

Summary Justice

This may have been a lonely, windswept heath, but the murder didn't go unobserved. Several people had seen the four men leave the inn at Thursley and, afterwards, two of them happened to be taking the self-same road. They saw the attack on the sailor, found his mutilated body, and hurried back to Thursley to raise the alarm. It wasn't long before Casey, Lonegon and Marshall were overtaken and arrested in the Sun Inn at Rake, near Petersfield.

The three murderers were held in Guildford Gaol until their trial at Kingston in April 1787, where they pleaded guilty to 'wilful murder and robbing'. Their total haul was valued at £1-7-6; just £1.38 in today's money.

Justice, it seems, was quicker in those days, for the three men were hung just two days later, close to the scene of their hideous crime. Then their bodies were coated in tar, and hung in chains from a great iron wheel mounted on top of a tall wooden post. The scene of the executions is still known as Gibbet Hill; it lies just a short way off your route, where a Celtic cross now stands on the summit.

Walk 47 Directions

① Cross the busy A3 at the car park entrance and turn left onto the waymarked track directly opposite. This is the old **Portsmouth Road**, which climbs imperceptibly away from its modern counterpart. Just before it starts to bend to the left,

look out for the sailor's memorial on the left-hand side. Now follow the old road around the left-hand bend, and drop gently back down to the A3.

② Take great care crossing here, then continue up the public byway opposite, waymarked '**Greensand Way**'. Continue along this rutted,

---

WHAT TO LOOK FOR ⓘ

About 100yds (91m) past the sailor's memorial you'll see a short, waymarked diversion to **Gibbet Hill** on your right-hand side. A Celtic cross stands near the old Ordnance Survey triangulation pillar at the top, and a plate points out views to places as far afield as Winchester and Windsor (26 miles/42km), Portsmouth (27 miles/43km), East Grinstead (30 miles/48km) and London (38 miles/61km). Bring your binoculars!

---

stony path for ½ mile (800m) until it drops to a cross-track at a waymark post on the edge of a belt of trees.

③ Turn left off the **Greensand Way** here, and bear gently right just beyond a second waymark post 60yds (55m) further on. The unsurfaced track is easy to follow as it winds down towards the youth hostel. Continue straight ahead as another track leads in from the right opposite a bench seat, enjoying the open views to the woodland across the valley. Keep straight on through the gate next to the cattle grid, signposted towards the **youth hostel**.

The track winds through mixed woodland, crosses a tiny stream at **Gnome Cottage**, then climbs steeply to a seat by a wooden gate. Turn right here through the gate, marked '**Pedestrian Path Youth Hostel and Hillcrest**'. A few paces beyond the youth hostel entrance

bear right along a woodland path that drops down to a small wooden footbridge. Cross the brook here, and make the short, sharp climb up the boggy sunken lane opposite.

④ Turn left at the top onto a delightful wooded track. Just around a left-hand bend keep to the lower, left-hand fork, waymarked '**Nature Trail**'. This is the start of ½ mile (800m) of steady, but unremitting ascent to the summit, where you'll join another lane near a pair of wooden gates. Turn right through the smaller gate and bear gently left, then right, for the last 125yds (114m) back to the **Hillcrest car park** where your walk began.

WHILE YOU'RE THERE ⓘ

Once described as a 'mini British Museum', **Haslemere's Educational Museum** covers everything from botany and zoology to archaeology and European folk art. Favourites include the bird migration display and an Egyptian mummy, but there are also things you wouldn't expect to find in a museum; a garden, a beehive where you can get up close and personal with the residents, and a daily display of fresh wild flowers. All this, plus events, lectures, and holiday activities for the kids. Open Tuesday to Saturday, 10AM–5PM.

WHERE TO EAT AND DRINK ⓘ

Tired, wet and somewhat bedraggled, you wouldn't normally find me heading for a 3-star hotel. Still, the **Devils Punchbowl** was just across the road from Hillcrest, so I gave their Russel Bar a try. What I found was a friendly welcome, a decent selection of beers, and a good range of lunchtime bar meals for under £5. Families, well behaved dogs – even dishevelled authors – are welcome here, so do pop in and give them my regards. Alternatively, the old Hillcrest café has been refurbished by the National Trust and reopened as the **Devil's Punch Bowl Café**.

A Pilgrimage to Waverley

By the enchanting ruins of Waverley Abbey in the Wey Valley.

•DISTANCE•	3 miles (4.8km)
•MINIMUM TIME•	1hr
•ASCENT / GRADIENT•	164ft (50m) ▲▲ ▲
•LEVEL OF DIFFICULTY•	🚶 🚶 🚶
•PATHS•	Sandy and easy to follow, two sections on minor roads
•LANDSCAPE•	Gently rolling, well-wooded countryside
•SUGGESTED MAP•	aqua3 OS Explorer 145 Guildford & Farnham
•START / FINISH•	Grid reference: SU 870455
•DOG FRIENDLINESS•	Generally good, but dogs must be on lead along roads
•PARKING•	Waverley Lane between Farnham and Elstead
•PUBLIC TOILETS•	None on route

BACKGROUND TO THE WALK

The glory of this walk lies right at the start, just a stone's throw across the fields from the car park. For over 400 years Waverley Abbey stood in this peaceful loop of the northern River Wey and, from here, its abbots wielded enormous religious and political influence. It all began in 1128 when William Gifford, the Bishop of Winchester, founded Waverley on 60 acres (24ha) of farmland. This was the first Cistercian abbey in England, and the original community of 12 monks came with Abbot John from L'Aumone in France. They lived an austere life, devoted to hard manual labour and unceasing prayer.

Spreading the Word

Construction started at once, although it was another 150 years before the abbey church was finally completed. Meanwhile the Cistercians expanded rapidly throughout Britain, and by 1132 there were great abbeys at Tintern, Fountains and Rievaulx. Waverley itself was the springboard for 13 new monasteries; in each case, an abbot and 12 monks, representing Christ and his 12 disciples, went forward as the nucleus of the new community.

At Waverley, as elsewhere, the monks had a significant impact on the local economy as they converted the surrounding forests into grazing and arable fields. They began Surrey's wool industry, and extended their hospitality from the humblest to the greatest. The lavish scale of monastic entertaining seems positively decadent, but these were exceptions to the harsh, everyday routine. Monks rose at 2AM for Matins, spending their time in meditation, study, and manual work before retiring as early as 5:30PM in winter. The day was punctuated by eight services, and by the midday meal of vegetables, bread and beer.

The monks ate in silence in the refectory, accompanied by readings from scripture. You'll see the remains of this building with its 13th-century vaulting during your visit; look, too, for the walls of the Chapter House, where the Abbot presided over the daily business meeting. Of the church itself, only the ground plan and some sections of the chancel walls remain to give you an idea of the scale of the building. The monastic community continued until it was suppressed by Henry VIII in 1536. The estate subsequently changed hands many times; over the years, the buildings were quarried for stone, and many wagon loads found their way into the construction of nearby Loseley House.

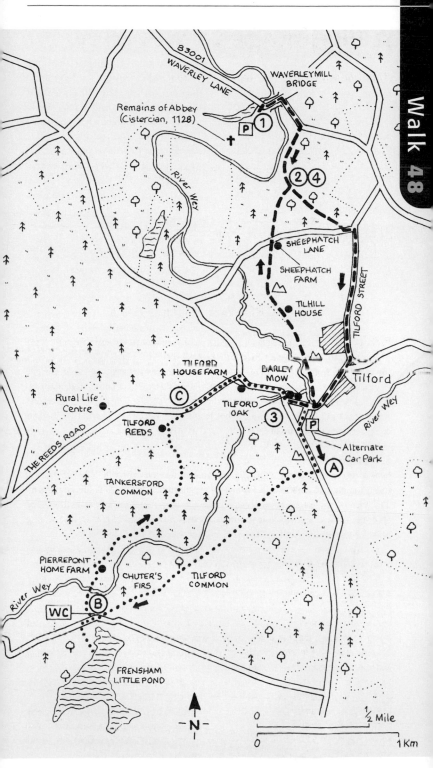

B3001

WAVERLEY LANE

WAVERLEYMILL BRIDGE

Remains of Abbey
(Cistercian, 1128)

P ①

River Wey

② ④

SHEEPHATCH LANE

SHEEPHATCH FARM

TILHILL HOUSE

TILFORD STREET

TILFORD HOUSE FARM

BARLEY MOW

Tilford

Rural Life Centre

TILFORD REEDS

TILFORD OAK

③

P

River Wey

THE REEDS ROAD

Ⓒ

Alternate Car Park

Ⓐ

TANKERSFORD COMMON

PIERREPONT HOME FARM

CHUTER'S FIRS

TILFORD COMMON

River Wey

WC

Ⓑ

FRENSHAM LITTLE POND

-N-

0   ½ Mile

0   1 Km

Walk 48 Directions

① Turn right out of the car park, taking care to watch out for traffic, and follow **Waverley Lane** (B3001) as it zig-zags left and right over **Waverleymill Bridge**. Continue for 200yds (183m) until the road bears to the left. Turn right here, onto the public byway, and follow it through to a metal gate and public byway signpost.

WHERE TO EAT AND DRINK ⓘ
Half way round your walk, relax in the whitewashed **Barley Mow**, delightfully situated overlooking Tilford's village green. There's cricket here in the summer – but you'll find a good choice of bar snacks and restaurant meals (except Sunday and Monday evenings).

② Keep straight ahead and follow the path past **Friars Way Cottage** until you come to **Sheephatch Lane**. Turn left briefly, then right at the junction with **Tilford Street**; there's no pavement for the first 400yds (366m), so go carefully. Now follow the road past the school, over the River Wey bridge and onto **Tilford village green**, where you'll find the **Tilford Oak** and welcome refreshment at the **Barley Mow**.

WHILE YOU'RE THERE ⓘ
Spread out over 10 acres (3.7ha) of field and woodland, **Tilford's Rural Life Centre** presents a vivid recreation of local country life over the last century and a half. You'll see realistic settings including everything from agriculture and hop growing to the rural post office and wheelwright's workshop. There's also a shop, café, picnic area and children's playground, and you can ride the **Old Kiln Light Railway** on Sundays and bank holidays. Open Wednesday to Sunday (and bank holidays), April to September.

③ To continue your walk, retrace your steps across the river bridge. Almost at once, turn left at the public bridleway sign just before the **Post Office**. The path climbs gently for 500yds (457m) and brings you to a tarmac lane. Turn left, pass **Tilhill House**, and continue up the narrow sandy track straight ahead. At the top of the short slope, fork right at the public bridleway waymark for the 400yds (366m) climb to **Sheephatch Farm**. Cross **Sheephatch Lane**, where a public byway sign points your way up the gravelled track directly opposite. The track leads you confidently through **Sheephatch Copse**, and soon you'll be dropping down through an ancient sunken way to rejoin your outward track at a metal gate and public byway signpost.

WHAT TO LOOK FOR ⓘ
Beside the green at Tilford, close to the Farnham road bridge, the **Tilford Oak** is said to be at least 800 years old. William Cobbett thought it the finest tree that he ever saw in his life, but now its branches have been lopped and the trunk is patched with iron sheets. In 1822, Cobbett claims that the tree was a full 30ft (10m) round, but his legendary enthusiasm may have run away with him. When the writer Eric Parker measured it in July 1907, its circumference was 24ft 9in (7.5m); he returned in 1934, and found it exactly 1ft (30cm) more. Just opposite this mighty specimen stands a mere sapling, planted in 1902 to commemorate Edward VII's coronation. At the opposite end of the green, its neighbour dates from Queen Victoria's Jubilee in 1897.

④ Turn left here for the easy walk back to **Waverley Lane** (B3001). Watch out for the traffic as you turn left, then retrace your outward route over **Waverleymill Bridge** and back to the car park.

A Frensham Loop

Enjoy this extension to Walk 48 by starting from Tilford village green.
See map and information panel for Walk 48

Walk 49

•DISTANCE•	3 miles (4.8km) (this loop only)
•MINIMUM TIME•	1hr 30min
•ASCENT / GRADIENT•	295ft (90m) ▲▲▲
•LEVEL OF DIFFICULTY•	🚶🚶 🚶🚶 🚶
•DOG FRIENDLINESS•	Not allowed on beaches around Frensham Pond, must be on lead through Pierrepont Home Farm

Walk 49 Directions
(Walk 48 option)

Leave the main route at Point ③ and walk up the left hand side of the green, passing the little car park on your left. Turn left at the top, signposted towards **Thursley and Hindhead**, and continue to the byway crossing at the top of the hill (Point Ⓐ).

Turn right onto the byway, fork left at the waymark post 100yds (91m) further on, and follow the track across **Tilford Common**. Cross the little footbridge at **Chuter's Firs**, and continue past the toilets on your right (Point Ⓑ).

Carry on across **Priory Lane**, bear left through the car park, and drop down the short slope to **Frensham Little Pond**.

Both the Frensham ponds were created in the Middle Ages, to supply the Bishop of Winchester's Court with fish during their stays at his palace in nearby Farnham. The area is now internationally important for its wildlife, and popular for sailing and fishing.

Retrace your steps to Point Ⓑ, and turn left at the toilets onto a bridleway. Cross the **River Wey**, and follow the path as it winds left and right around the mellow brick buildings of **Pierrepont Home Farm**. Leave the farmyard through an old iron gate and, after 30yds (27m), take the left hand fork that plunges into the woodlands of **Tankersford Common**. An easy walk brings you to the secluded hamlet of **Tilford Reeds**, where your path swings right onto a gravelled drive for the final section to the **Reeds Road** (Point Ⓒ).

> **WHAT TO LOOK FOR** ⓘ
> Keep your eyes peeled on Tankersford Common for a glimpse of a **green woodpecker**. The largest British woodpecker, you won't mistake this conspicuous, bright green bird with its crimson cap and yellow rump. Although it excavates its own nesting hole, the green woodpecker also spends a lot of time on the ground, probing for insects with its long, pointed beak.

Follow the road to the junction at **Tilford House Farm**, and turn right. There's rather more traffic on this road, so do take care on your way back to **Tilford** village green. Turn left onto the green, and rejoin the main walk at Point ③.

Walk 50

Farnham Town Trail

A relaxed, flexible walk through 800 years of Farnham's history.

•DISTANCE•	3¾ miles (6km)
•MINIMUM TIME•	2hrs
•ASCENT / GRADIENT•	328ft (100m)
•LEVEL OF DIFFICULTY•	
•PATHS•	Paved streets and country park trails, can be muddy
•LANDSCAPE•	Attractive market town in informal parkland setting
•SUGGESTED MAP•	aqua3 OS Explorer 145 Guildford & Farnham or 'Historic Farnham', from tourist information centre in South Street
•START / FINISH•	Grid reference: SU 837475
•DOG FRIENDLINESS•	Good in Farnham Park, not so good in busy town centre
•PARKING•	Farnham Park, just off Castle Hill, Farnham
•PUBLIC TOILETS•	Farnham Park and the Hart, near Upper Hart car park

Walk 50 **Directions**

Farnham Park was enclosed around 1376 as one of the two deer parks belonging to the Bishops of Winchester. Parliamentary troops were billeted here during the Civil War and, more recently, the Women's Land Army grew food crops in the park during the Second World War. Nowadays you'll find playing fields and a public golf course, but most of the park is simply informal countryside.

You can wander at will in the park, or try this circuit. Bear right out of the car park, and walk up the long avenue of trees until you reach the buildings in the south east corner of the park. Turn left onto a tarmac path, cross the brook, and continue under the power lines to the information board near the park entrance at **Upper Hale**. Turn left again, onto another tarmac path that runs diagonally across the park, back under the power lines and past the **Ranger's House**. You'll cross your outward track within sight of the car park, before the path leads you down out of the park along a little alley that comes out into **Park Row**. Turn right here, then left into **Castle Street**. On your left you'll pass an attractive row of brick almshouses, built in 1619 'for the habitation and relief of eight poor honest old impotent persons'. I wonder how the residents feel about that description today?

WHILE YOU'RE THERE   ⓘ

Henry of Blois founded **Farnham Castle** in 1138, and it remained an official residence for the Bishops of Winchester until the Diocese of Guildford was created in 1927. Henry's successors strengthened the original castle by degrees, and added the Palace at the foot of the 12th-century Keep. You'll get some great views of the town from the Keep, which is just a few minutes walk down Castle Hill from Farnham Park. It's open daily, between April and October. The former Palace is open for guided tours all year round, on Wednesday afternoons only.

Walk 50

Continue to the bottom of **Castle Street**, where the small fruit and vegetable market trades every weekday on the site of the old timber framed market house that stood here between 1566 and 1866. Cross the road and turn left into **The Borough**, but spare a few minutes here to browse the small specialist shops in **Borelli Yard**, where you'll also see *The Matriarch* sculpture by Ben Franklin.

Charles Borelli was a jeweller by trade, but in the early years of the 20th century he bought and restored several of Farnham's more interesting old buildings. He worked closely with local architect Harold Falkner, and the two men collaborated on the colonnaded **Town Hall Buildings**, now one of Farnham's best known landmarks on the corner of **Castle Street** and **The Borough**.

Turn right into **South Street**, cross the river, then turn right into **Gostrey Meadow**. The path leads you back across a footbridge over the river; bear left through the gardens, then cross **Longbridge** and continue along the riverside path with the **Maltings** across the water on your left. Bear right through the

car park to the New Ashgate Gallery, then turn left into **Lower Church Lane**. Continue into **St Andrew's churchyard**, and follow the cobbled path past the west door and up the narrow lane signposted towards the museum.

You'll come out into **West Street**, opposite the post office. Cross at the lights, turn right for 100yds (91m), then turn left through the arch into **Lion and Lamb Yard**. At the top, you'll come to Safeway's; turn left under the colonnade, bear right through **Upper Hart** car park, and take the brick paved footpath up between **Farnham Baptist Church** and the **Art College**. Continue past the **Porters' Lodge**, up the steps and out of the college campus.

Keep straight on, up a few rustic steps and through a couple of small fields to a waymark post. Bear right here, down a narrow path that leads you between fences and out into **Old Park Lane**. Turn right, cross **Castle Hill**, then turn left onto the railed roadside footpath. Pass Farnham Cricket Club, and turn right at the signposted entrance to **Farnham Park** where your walk began.

Walking in Safety

All these walks are suitable for any reasonably fit person, but less experienced walkers should try the easier walks first. Route finding is usually straightforward, but you will find that an Ordnance Survey map is a useful addition to the route maps and descriptions.

Risks

Although each walk here has been researched with a view to minimising the risks to the walkers who follow its route, no walk in the countryside can be considered to be completely free from risk. Walking in the outdoors will always require a degree of common sense and judgement to ensure that it is as safe as possible.

- Be particularly careful on cliff paths and in upland terrain, where the consequences of a slip can be very serious.

- Remember to check tidal conditions before walking on the seashore.

- Some sections of route are by, or cross, busy roads. Take care and remember traffic is a danger even on minor country lanes.

- Be careful around farmyard machinery and livestock, especially if you have children with you.

- Be aware of the consequences of changes in the weather and check the forecast before you set out. Carry spare clothing and a torch if you are walking in the winter months. Remember the weather can change very quickly at any time of the year, and in moorland and heathland areas, mist and fog can make route finding much harder. Don't set out in these conditions unless you are confident of your navigation skills in poor visibility. In summer remember to take account of the heat and sun; wear a hat and carry spare water.

- On walks away from centres of population you should carry a whistle and survival bag. If you do have an accident requiring the emergency services, make a note of your position as accurately as possible and dial 999.

Acknowledgements

Dozens of people have helped me with researching this book. The staff of libraries, tourist information offices and attractions throughout Surrey have all done their bit, and chance acquaintances have put me on the trail of things I would never have found on my own.

I'd also like to thank each of the following people who have gone out of their way to make my job just that little bit easier. Brian Angove (Epsom Downs Racecourse), Nick Channer (Outdoor Writers' Guild), John Cook (Hampton Ferry), Gordon Flower (Headley Heath National Trust Warden), Rhian French (Ordnance Survey), Margaret Griffiths (Surrey History Service), David Hiscock (North Downs Way Project Manager), Susan Knowles (BBC Written Archives Centre), Mike Marshall (Beaverbrook Foundation), David Peek (Haxted Mill), Sheila Thomas (Outwood Windmill), Bobbie Thompson (Leith Hill National Trust shop), Philippa Wadsworth (National Trust Press Office), Revd DA Wotton (Rector of Headley). As usual though, the biggest debt is to my wife, Sue, for her long-suffering patience and support.

David Foster

Series management: Outcrop Publishing Services, Cumbria
Series editor: Chris Bagshaw
Front cover: AA Photo Library/John Miller